WOMEN PREFER WOMEN

by

ELULA PERRIN

TRANSLATED FROM THE FRENCH BY HAROLD J. SALEMSON

WILLIAM MORROW AND COMPANY, INC.
NEW YORK 1979

Library of Congress Cataloging in Publication Data

Perrin, Elula.
Women prefer women.

Translation of Les femmes préfèrent les femmes.
1. Perrin, Elula. 2. Lesbians —France— Biography. I. Title.
HQ75.4.P47A3413 301.41'57'0924 78-13330
ISBN 0-688-03407-1

BOOK DESIGN CARL WEISS

Printed in the United States of America.

First Edition

1 2 3 4 5 6 7 8 9 10

Natalie [*Barney*] *is a pure daughter of Eve. Adam does not seem to have been involved in her conception. Men—her father, cousins, suitors, friends—are only very far-off worshipers who live on another planet. Natalie loved only women, spontaneously, openly, at a time when hypocrisy and convention reigned all-powerfully. Thus did she become the first liberated woman of her time.*

"She was irresistible as are all those women who have followed their own nature. She is irresistible as are all those women who have dared to live. . . ."

—JEAN CHALON
Portrait d'une séductrice

WOMEN PREFER WOMEN

CHAPTER

I

She lay down on top of me. Strange, that this frail, light body did not crush me. We kissed till we couldn't breathe, as we had the day before. Her hands began to caress me. That was sweet, light—two birds' wings grazing my breasts, my hips, my thighs, my belly.

Our vulvas one against the other, as if cheek to cheek, nothing between.

The sensation of this fleece caressing mine . . .

A hand slipping between us, seeking me out, finding me immediately and touching me, becoming insistent. I melt, I liquefy.

Her mouth leaves mine, slides along my neck, to my shoulder, surrounding my breasts delicately. All the while her hand holds me tense, in suspense. I know what is coming. I know that her lips are going to come to rest on my belly, that soon her tongue will replace that soft skillful hand. And this gesture—so hard to accept from Guy, because I was ashamed of it, because it made me ill at ease, because my vagina then became a cesspool of drooling salivation in which a thick fat tongue moved about without direction, because it moved in too many directions—this sudden gesture is what I desire with all my being. Her tongue takes the place of her hand without interrupting the beat, without breaking the tension.

Sweet, skillful, I feel her on me and suddenly the heat of her entire mouth swallows me up. Her tongue almost hurts and her lips soothe the fire—hot—heat—thrill—I hear myself moan. This is the first time. With Guy, I just pretended. Now I surprise myself and listen to myself, amazed.

No longer do I have to ask, "When you have an orgasm, what is it like?" No longer do I fear that I am reaching a point where I will bump into a closed door. The door is open wide, like my thighs, like my belly, like my mouth crying out!

And suddenly, I feel invaded. She is inside me, huger, realer, deeper than Guy's penis.

The magic of feeling sated, fulfilled, the wildness of no longer knowing what is making me cry out this way—her tongue or her lips or her fingers. I tremble, I shake my head every which way, and only feel dizzier.

I open my eyes. Far away, down there, between my legs, are two tender eyes watching my orgasm, hair that I can take hold of, cheeks (oh so sweet) that I caress with my palms. A woman is making love to me. A woman is making me come. At last.

At last, yes, this was it, what I had been waiting for, had been looking for. Moustique, ordinary woman, woman I am not in love with, object-woman, teacher-woman, without involving my heart, or my head, or my love, or my tenderness, you taught me how to make love. You brought the first shout, you delivered me into pleasure, into orgasm. The flame has caught, alone, in the pit of my stomach, I finally become conscious that I have a clitoris and that it is throbbing like a dying bird.

I am born at last to love. I had waited twenty-one years . . . A woman at last—at last like other women.

How far I had to journey to reach this clearing, the pure air, the sun of the flower-women, the fruit-women, runaway-women, sorrow-women.

That is how I became a lesbian in Casablanca one afternoon in March 1950, in a cheap hotel room. This second birth was as important for me as the first.

Why am I writing about this? Why am I confessing all this? Because for the last nine years I have reigned over the night life of those nasty ladies, the homosexual women, dykes, butches—all those cute names we are sometimes called.

"The girls at the Katmandou are the most beautiful in Paris, as beautiful as the ones at Castel's and Régine's."

That claim did not originate with me; all the Paris-by-Night guidebooks proclaim it.

Every evening, elegantly dressed women and pretty girls come to dance, to flirt, to talk, to have a drink at my place. They are the women I have loved my whole life. Yes, I am a lesbian. I love woman, women, passionately, profoundly, exclusively. And by the greatest of luck, the purest of chance, that profession of faith has turned out to be my profession as well.

I live every night among these women I love, and since they are the ones I make my living from, I feel blessed with extraordinary luck! My professional life and my personal life are wonderfully at one. And I for one never need to hide the fact that I'm a lesbian, since I am one of the best known. . . . I never have to hide, as most of my sisters do. And not only don't I have to hide, but every night I talk about us; I explain us, defend us, I try to plead our poorly understood cause to those few men admitted to the sanctum sanctorum.

We are the least known of those who are out of the ordinary, those who are the peripheral creatures of the sexual world.

The literature about us is meager indeed: ten or so valid novels, and in the textbooks on medicine, psychiatry, and sex there is a single chapter, usually terse, fleshless, devoid of living examples, covering only a few purely pathological cases. And even then, it is stuck in between the case of a gentleman who makes a fetish of high-laced shoes and another who loves to have his back whipped.

We are the Jivaros of the extranormals. The stupidest beliefs, the most threadbare clichés about us, are what I would like to destroy. I would like to demystify and demythologize us. We are not a race apart. We are women, in every sense of the word. We are neither ugly ducklings unredeemed by conquering males, nor depraved perverts taking our pleasures only in the shadows of hidden doorways, as is the case with certain male homosexuals.

Who are we? What are we searching for in life, in love, in pleasure? Maybe the best way to find out is to take one of us and dissect her. I may as well be that little frog for the sake of science. My life is in no way exemplary; yet it may lift some of the shadows and allow us to be better understood.

So—here I come.

I come into being in Hanoi, then still the capital of Tonkin, French Indochina, in March 1929. A fine year! The great depression may have been starting, but that was the best of years for great vintages, as well as for my parents, who had been hoping and waiting for me since they got married three years before.

My mother was a frail little mixed-breed who stood just under five feet, and my father was a violent Maltese, born in Tunisia, six foot four. An oddly matched couple who got along together very poorly. My father shouted, beat the native boys and coolies, cheated on my mother with every one of her girl friends he could, and gave me memorable spankings. The house was always filled with people and noise.

My three young uncles lived with us, as well as my father's mother. She was an Italian from Tunis, truculent, blustering, running the whole household from her rattan chair, where she sat paralyzed. All day long she stayed in that one spot, for she would not hear of having a wheelchair. I would climb up on her lap and listen over and over again to the fabulous stories she told, French fairy tales improved and spiced up with details from the Arabian Nights and sprinkled with Italian and Arabic words, and ghost stories, too, and tales of the phantoms and spirits with whom she maintained constant—if unfriendly—relations.

My little nursemaids, my *thi-haïs,* in order to get me to sleep at night, whispered awful stories to me in their Annamite tongue, about *ma-cui,* the devil, and evil spirits. It was hard to fall asleep alone after all that! I slept in my parents' bedroom and was sometimes rudely awakened by my shouting father as he threatened my mother with a revolver.

For he was not only violent, he was a troublemaker and a womanizer. He was also horrendously jealous.

I adored that father of mine. He was Zeus thundering from high on Olympus. When he carried me on his shoulders, in the Botanical Garden, where he took me to see the monkeys and tigers, or in Rue Paul-Bert at apéritif time in the Taverne Royale, I was Queen of Hanoi and the Petit-Lac.

Yet things had begun badly between us. Just two days after I was born, ornery already, I turned night into day and cried so loud my poor mother couldn't sleep. So my father wrapped me in a blanket, carted me home, and dumped me on my grandmother's bed like a load of dirty laundry, saying, "Here, take this. Don't let me hear any more about it!"

Mother's father was a mining engineer. He had come to Tonkin around 1900, with two of his brothers, one an engineer like him, the other an officer in the colonial infantry.

At that time, white women were at a premium. There were not even the fancy whorehouse mademoiselles yet, such as the ones in high-priced Saigon among whom a whole generation of gentlemen-settlers found themselves wives that they made respectable and inevitably holier-than-thou.

So all three Perrin brothers took on Annamite concubines, by whom they had whole strings of children. The two engineers, laid low by the fevers of Upper Tonkin and Yunnan, soon died, each leaving three or four kids. The concubines, the fathers of their children scarcely out of sight, lost no time in disappearing in turn. Maternal instinct is not overwhelming among the Annamites. They abandoned the little bastards. And the major took them all in and raised them all, sending the girls to school with the "good sisters" and the boys to Lycée Albert-Sarraut. They all turned out to be doctors or engineers, the girls married nice guys; in a word, they were real lucky little yellow bastards!

Mother ran a very fancy dress shop, where the Frenchwomen from Hanoi's high society came to have copies made of the latest Paris creations. I spent my childhood among yard goods, spangles, braid, fancy buttons, and laces. I used to take some to school with me to swap for marbles or books. I had only one doll, and a boy doll at that, a little swimmer who, as years went by, became a great invalid, pieced together with rubber bands and adhesive tape. It did no good to give me pretty dolls; they bored me silly. They looked stupid. I preferred toy soldiers and the blue racing car I pedaled for hours up and down the verandas.

Fittings. What torture! I was the best-dressed little girl in Hanoi, for sure, with my couturière mother. But I hated it! I would whine, get sick to my stomach, dizzy from having to stand motionless while the master cutter, the apprentice cutter, the assistant cutter, and the little native boy who picked up the pins all whirled about me.

"Turn around! Stand straight! Don't move! You'll never know how to wear clothes, my girl!"

Mother knocked herself out. She cut my eyelashes while I was asleep so they would grow back fuller and curlier, and twice I had my head shaved to make my hair come in heavier and wavy. I must say there is little left to show for it . . . And the second time it caused me real humiliation, because with my bare skull I was taken for a little boy, which made me absolutely furious.

I was so impossible at home, they tell me, that just as soon as I could say *pipi* and *caca*—the only two warning words considered an entrance requirement—I was sent to school. I was two and a half. Mother went with me and gave me a big checkered handkerchief that she shoved into the pocket of my rompers.

It was the first day of school, September 15. She kissed me and told me to be very good. I stayed sitting at my place, very quietly. And then I realized that all the kids around me were bawling, screaming, and desperately hanging on to their mothers' skirts. I felt I ought to do the same. So I took out my big kerchief and started to sob too.

I immediately became a very good schoolgirl, obedient, disciplined, and quiet. I liked school a lot. When I got home, I would make a beeline for my grandmother. She was unnaturally prone to catastrophe: ceiling fans tended to fall down on her, and hunks of the ceiling as well. Glasses tinkled on their own, thermos bottles exploded, even when there were none of those little temblors that are so frequent in Tonkin. Hers was a strange world, full of signals from the Great Beyond . . .

In Indochina, little kids run around naked, so the sex difference was never any secret to me. Boys had their little faucet in front, but girls didn't. I didn't know how adults were made, and couldn't have cared less.

I must have been six when my little native nursemaid who was then taking care of me first showed me how to play doctor. She was probably sixteen or seventeen. We played it for hours, during siesta time, when the whole house was napping. She would stretch out on the floor, on a mat, and take off her black trousers, beneath which she was naked. I examined her at length. Her slit was pink, almost red, like the behinds of the monkeys I saw in the Botanical Garden, and it didn't have any hairs. I ran my fingers around in it, and then she would set me up straddling her, and rub herself against my own bump, for by this time I had rolled down my panties, too. She moved faster and faster and then suddenly she would pant a little and let out a sigh. I don't know what she was feeling. All I got out of it was a feeling of disgust.

I would smell the stale odor that she had left on my fingers and promise myself that this was the last time. But in a few days there we were doing it again, whoever's idea it was.

When I was seven and had reached the age of reason, I wrote to Father Christmas sometime in the course of the year to ask for a little brother. I did it absolutely secretly, addressed the envelope, as is the custom, to "Father Christmas in Heaven," and sneaked off to mail it myself.

The next day I caught it from everyone in the house (but kindly). It seemed you were not supposed to write to Father Christmas out of season. Fortunately, Hanoi was a small town, the postman had opened the letter, and a woman friend of my parents' had brought it back to them. They all had a lot of fun out of it. But nonetheless a few months later I did get the little brother I had wished for. I had apparently been alone in my wish, for my parents were at the time in the process of getting a divorce.

My mother was fed up with his sleeping with all of her friends and customers. And from one violent outbreak to the next, our family was coming apart at the seams. My mother, being pregnant, stayed on in Hanoi, where she continued to run her shop. My grandmother and I left for Haiphong, where my father was to be in charge of the Boy Landry Company, an export-import firm.

We had a big apartment above the store with three covered terraces that seemed gigantic to me. I spent my best, most dreamy years there in the midst of ten or twelve cats and dogs.

During siesta time, now that I no longer had a young woman companion, I became a bold, brave knight, tirelessly riding on a railing that had become my favorite charger and rescuing damsels in distress.

But no more off-color games. At a tea party two of my

little friends, Monique and Simone, had started to play doctor. I left in a hurry and for years, until we graduated, I could not look at them without distaste.

At Haiphong, I fell in love for the first time—with my schoolteacher. To be more truthful, it was for the second time. The first had been with one of my mother's customers, a gorgeous blonde married to a Chinese millionaire. When she came for fittings, I would hide behind a screen so as to be able to drink in her good looks. I was hopelessly in love, and would say, "When I grow up, I'm going to marry Madame Nam Sang." Everybody thought that was very funny and awfully cute.

My teacher was a very pretty young brunette who lived with her sisters. I carried a torch for her all year long. For her birthday, I made the whole class chip in to buy her a present that I picked out myself. I don't remember what it was, but it cost a lot and I was very proud of myself. Giving a present to a teacher was something unheard of, and she was so delighted that she invited us all over for tea. I was her pet, of course, and besides, I was always at the head of the class.

The year before, on the other hand, I had had my first real shock. A short time before Christmas, the teacher had given us a composition to write: "What Do You Want for Christmas?" adding: "You are all old enough to realize, of course, that there is no Father Christmas, and it is your parents who buy the presents." I was dumbfounded!

I should point out that I was about two years younger than most of the girls in the class. I felt very sorry for that teacher, with her hair that had already turned white, and no illusions left. I felt the kind of tender pity for her that a believer has toward an atheist. *I* of course knew that there really was a Father Christmas: for proof, look at the little brother I had ordered out of season and gotten just the same. So, no use trying to kid me about old Father Christmas.

I wrote my composition, serenely, my belief intact and it was only the following year that my father told me—at mealtime the day after Christmas—that if I was counting on Father Christmas to bring me what I wanted I had a long wait in store. It was a real shock. All my beliefs crumbled at one blow: the Tooth Fairy, Father Christmas, and just everything . . .

But for all that, even today (alas! or thank God!—I'm not sure which), I still believe in Santa Claus, and I always trust people fully and without reservation . . .

After Haiphong, Papa went back to Hanoi. He was often away, crisscrossing Tonkin for the Boy Landry Company, and I often stayed alone with my grandmother. We lived in a big dark four-storied house, but occupied only the ground floor. Ah! How I hated those huge soulless colonial manses, made to house cheap furniture—for the termites and woodworms made no distinction between an eighteenth-century escritoire and a 1930 catchall. I was afraid everywhere, the minute I got away from the family hearth, represented by my grandmother's bed and chair, and my own room that was always right next to hers. The other rooms seemed empty to me, as if abandoned by us and now taken over by evil spirits. The atmosphere in them was heavy: spirits still played a big part in our daily life.

I remember a square table, with copper-handled drawers, that my father and grandmother condemned to ritual burning after a family council. It brought us bad luck, they said.

The native boys hacked it to pieces and burned it in the yard. The copper handles were thrown into the trash along with the ashes. I don't know whether the curse was broken, but a short time later my grandmother had to be operated on for cataracts.

I was sent to spend a month with some friends, whose father was the warden of the Hanoi Prison. It was just across from the Palace of Justice. We would come home from the lycée and knock at the heavy door. A peephole opened, hinges creaked, and our steps and joyful shouts could be heard echoing through the long dark corridors.

I shared the bedroom with the three daughters of the jailer. The windows looked out on the women's yard. Watching them exercise was exciting. My hostesses were used to it, but I would hang on to the bars unable to take my eyes off the women in gray trousers and jackets, jabbering, fighting, screaming in the enclosure below me. I was fascinated: to think they were criminals, thieves, maybe murderesses, too . . . They didn't frighten me. Sometimes they looked up toward our windows, but they remained indifferent.

On the other hand, from the kitchen you could see down into the men's yard. They shook their fists at us and spat out insults. If they ever rioted, they'd let us have it! Since I could understand Annamite, their threats haunted the nights I spent at the prison.

On Sundays, we went to mass. Until then, my religious training had been rather neglected. I had been baptized, my grandmother had taught me a few prayers, but that was all.

My father was a Freemason. I would see him go out at night with a fine embroidered red satin apron that was magnificent. He was grand master of his lodge and promised that when I was fifteen I'd join the Masonic "lewises."

So going to mass was an unusual diversion. I liked it a lot. We went to the cathedral, to the ten o'clock high mass.

Everyone was very well dressed, and there were choirs made up of the sisters' pupils; coming out, we would stop on the square, to talk, say hello to friends, and then go down Rue Paul-Bert and around the Petit-Lac. We would pester the flower vendors to give us their wilted lotuses, because the hearts, which looked like watering-can spouts, were full of deliciously chewable seeds. Then we took rickshaws back to the prison. It was like the Spanish Paseo. We were showing ourselves off to the others and watching them show off. The girls counted up the number of fellows who had given them the eye or smiled at them. That was their main concern. They could talk about it for hours on end, and all they dreamed of was what the next Sunday would be like.

I didn't have any "crushes." No list of fellows, no collection of furtive smiles. It made me seem like a jerk! So I chose one as a last resort. He was in the sixth grade, the same class I was in, his name was Paul, a good-looking little blond, toward the tail end of the class, when I was always at the head.

This charming boy never knew anything of the "love" I lavished on him all that school year. We never smiled at each other and he never took any interest in me, but as far as my girl friends were concerned he was my fellow, and a real good-looking guy, too! My honor was saved; I hadn't lost face.

My face, however, was no great shakes. Dark, my hair straight as a stick, on the skinny side, with long legs and a huge mouth, awkward, clumsy, hating sports and violent games, dreamy, indiscriminately devouring the Divine Aretino, Victor Hugo's *Légende des siècles*, Baudelaire's *Flowers of Evil*—at eleven I had no love on the horizon and the candidates weren't falling over each other . . .

My mother had remarried, this time to my godfather. They lived in Annam, and he was the head of a bank at Tourane, later to be known as Da Nang. I spent almost all my vacations with them, and those were the best times because I idolized my little brother. I saved all my pocket money to buy him the nicest gifts I could. On the other hand, I would pinch him and rough him up over practically nothing, when he didn't do exactly as I expected. Adoring and tyrannical . . . already . . .

And then came the war. The Japanese invaded Indochina peacefully, or practically so, after the incidents at Langson. The French administration carried on as usual, but now we saw battalions of macaques crossing Indochina on their way to Burma or Singapore. I remember their smell, the smell of their paper, their uniforms, their food, strangely the same, persistent, at once sweet and musky. They were not aggressive and adored children. One night, as I was going to see my mother at Tourane, and was to take the train alone, my father entrusted me to a compartment full of Japanese soldiers. During the night, I woke up wrapped in a khaki cover. They had covered the little white girl, and in the morning they shared their breakfast with me; rice and canned corned beef, which we called monkey meat when I was little. I had long refused to touch it, because I really believed that was what it was, and since I loved the monkeys in the zoo . . .

My father now lived at Thakhek in Laos, my mother in Annam; there was no longer any reason for me to be left alone in Hanoi. So I was sent to the Dominican Sisters' boarding school at Than Hoa in North Annam.

What fabulous women! Half of the community were Anglo-Saxons. These nuns taught us baseball and played soccer with us. I was always goalie, because I still had no taste for sports.

But I was taking piano lessons. The teacher was named Sister Marie-Agnès. She was French-Canadian, had taken first piano prize at the Quebec Conservatory, and was ugly as sin. She was the one who made the first advances and seduced me. It was a tender, fiery affair. She would hold me in her arms during the piano lessons and, to make it sound right, play with one hand while I snuggled up to her, my head buried in her veil; for the study hall was right next to the music room, and the piano could not be allowed to remain silent. On Sundays, at the parish mass, when she was the one to chaperone us, I stayed alongside her and during the whole service she would keep my hand in hers, under her blue-bordered white vestment. She would tell me about Canada, her childhood, and snow, and music, which was her passion.

Finally, her superiors must have been offended by our happy dream, for she was transferred to Upper Tonkin. Our farewell was wrenching. It was my first broken heart. I sobbed like a fool the morning she left after hugging me one last time. The world was collapsing. There was nothing left, no more of the warmth, the tenderness, the embrace of the mother that Sister Marie-Agnès had been to me. For my mother had never shown me such signs of tenderness, sweetness, warmth. My mother was a pretty Eurasian lady who played bridge, gave glamorous parties, and adored my little brother . . .

In class, in study hall, I had trouble holding back my tears, but stifled my sobs, bending over my Latin translation. That lasted several weeks. But since my heart already couldn't live with the void, Sister Sainte-Floride filled in. She was from New Zealand, dry, cold, severe, but an excellent teacher, feared and respected. She could not awaken love in me, nor did she try. Entirely given over to God, blameless even in her passions, she turned her obvious attraction for me into a religious vocation. For a whole year, just to make her happy, I was determined to become a nun like her. Her coldness almost became tenderness when she spoke of the love of God. Every night before going to sleep I recited the prayer to Saint Cecilia for receiving the vocation: "I love Christ who has called me to be his bride." That was really the only time that for a full year my heart beat over a man—and the results were not very convincing . . .

I had a sidekick: Marie-Thérèse, a sixteen-year-old with hairy legs, a short haircut, and a fine bass voice that stood out in the choir. She had been expelled from the Couvent des Oiseaux on account of some letters she had written to another student, whom she referred to as her little wife. At our school, she seduced Mother Marie-André, a young nun who was rather pretty and very lively. Our beds were alongside each other in the dormitory and of an evening or morning, when Mother Marie-André was on duty, she would raise the mosquito netting and bend over Marie-Thérèse, while they cooed to each other at length and kissed full on the mouth. This did not shock me, for Marie-Thérèse, who had lost her mother, said that that was the way she used to kiss her, and Mother Marie-André reminded her so much of her own dear mother that, in a word, it all seemed quite normal.

After a few months, however, this Marie-Thérèse started getting on my nerves. Her rough manners, her unfeminine movements, her boasting, her lying, became more than I could stand. And maybe it was on account of Nicole.

Nicole had a woman's body already, long wavy black hair, and she was beautiful and dumb. If Marie-Thérèse was in the tenth grade at sixteen, Nicole was fourteen and in the eighth. Nothing overbright about either one of them.

At first, she made advances toward me. Her hair smelled like grass when she put her head on my shoulder during recess. And then little by little, she entered into big Marie-Thérèse's sphere of influence. Our relations turned bitter-sweet. Soon I wasn't talking to her any more. She also took piano lessons with Mother Marie-Agnès's replacement. She rehearsed in the refectory and had tamed a little gray mouse that would come to listen to her play; she had named it Rodrigue. One day when Nicole was away, I convinced the monitor sister that that mouse had to be hunted down. Tallyho, Rodrigue! We closed the refectory, and after quite a hectic chase we killed the beastie.

When Nicole got back and learned about the massacre, she burst into tears. That evening, in the dormitory, she came over to me, still sobbing, and said, "Why did you do it? What did I ever do to you, to make you be so mean to me?"

I broke away from her sharply. I had no answer to give her, and perhaps I didn't really feel all that comfortable with myself . . .

Thereupon, I fell in love with Ginette. It was the end of the tenth grade, my last year at Than Hoa. We had a wonderful idyll. We went as far as holding hands! And the last big day, when I had hidden in the broom closet to cry my heart out before leaving, she came there to say goodbye and kissed me on the neck. It was warm. I was moist with sweat, and this kiss upset me. It was the most daring act of my whole boarding-school career.

I left Than Hoa regretfully. I had spent three wonderful

years there. Yet my parents were far away and I would see only one or the other of them at vacation time. But the discipline was not strict, the nuns were terrific, and the girls nice.

To be sure, I was always one of the best students. That took no great doing on my part, for I loved all my subjects, with the sole exception of math—in any form whatever.

I put on little shows for the entire community and they made a big thing of coming to applaud us in the refectory, even the novices and lay sisters. I loved theater. At Christmas and at the end of the school year, we would play scenes from the classics. I was Hermione, Bélise, Athalie, Louis XI, and Joan of Arc. I could not make up my mind between theater and medicine. Both vocations were equally attractive to me.

I had just gotten my *brevet* diploma * and was going on. If I had to leave Than Hoa, it was because classes there did not go any higher.

No more Thursday and Sunday outings in the wonderful Tonkinese countryside, among the rice paddies, the pagodas, the little villages snuggled alongside ponds in which little black pigs and gray water buffaloes wallowed. No more of the big bamboo waterwheels operated by foot by *nga-quês* in black pants and brown jackets, nor skillful potters who let us place the bowls on the throwing head and gave us fabulous hard-clay marbles that we played endless games with at recess.

I was about to enter an entirely different world at Dalat, at the Convent of the Birds.

But for now, summer vacation meant leaving Ginette.

Mother lived at Quang Ngnaï in a magnificent villa, a bit outside the city, right in among the sugarcane fields. During siesta, we would go out and cut some down with machetes. My little brother spent his days riding the water buffaloes with their little herders and spoke Vietnamese better than I. He in turn had a young lady companion around the same

* Equivalent to finishing two years of high school.

age; I don't know whether he was acquainted with the same games I had been taught.

Still entirely pure in spirit, I wrote Ginette passionate, exalted, flaming letters tens of pages long. I slept with her picture under my pillow so as to kiss her last thing at night and first thing in the morning.

She answered with dull letters, so awfully banal, and even somewhat apprehensive of my ardor, that when I saw her again a month later at Dalat, I said a forced hello to her and quickly turned away.

Anyway, I was now in a wholly different universe that fascinated me. The girls at Than Hoa had been the daughters of petty bureaucrats, customs men, small colonists. At Dalat, they were the *ne plus ultra*, the nieces of Emperor Bao Daï, the daughters of *Résidents*, mandarins, and big plantation owners. Cochin China was nearby, and that was where the big fortunes were.

Even the nuns were different: more cultured, more intellectual. We put on Paul Claudel's plays *The Hostage* and *The Tidings Brought to Mary*. We listened to classical music in a pavilion on the immense grounds. One evening, caught unawares by the sudden Asian nightfall, even though it always came at the same time, we heard the *cup-cup* of a tiger terrifyingly close by. It had been roaming in the neighborhood for several days and had been seen by one of the guards. There were ten or more of us, dying of fright, around a nun who was no braver than we, and we stayed locked in the pavilion until people came to rescue us, armed with flashlights and guns.

At night, it was almost cold. The way it is in France, that France that I dreamed about more and more—I, the quadroon, never popular, not always fit to be associated with considering my touch of yellow blood.

I remember the day, in kindergarten, when Mother told me she was coming to see the teacher. On those days, the kids were always proud: they would point out their mothers to their schoolmates and feel more important because they knew the mothers were there to talk about them.

I was proud, too. I announced to everyone that my mother was coming. She came in while we were still at recess. She was beautiful, elegant, made up, with lightly wavy auburn hair and carefully polished long nails.

"That's my mommy, that's my mommy!" I shouted.

One little girl looked at her, and then said to me, scornfully, "Why, your mommy's a half-breed!"

Some of the girls in my classes had simply never invited me to tea at their homes because of Mother's mixed blood.

But at the Convent of the Birds, there was no such problem. Money made equals of us all.

My father had done very well. He had a rice mill, trucks, boats, charcoal works that produced fuel for *gazogènes*. He had married a kind of nymphet who was as flat-chested as a boy—a nymphomaniac, if public rumor was to be trusted—with two daughters slightly younger than I.

I hated her. Since there was ever-increasing talk about possible revolt, or rioting, among the "natives," when I was on vacation at Thakhek, at my father's, I would sleep with a knife under my pillow, dreaming of how, if the revolt came, I could stab my stepmother and blame it on the rioters . . .

I still adored my father as much as ever, though I saw so little of him. He took me for two- and three-day trips in his trucks, to Laos and Upper Tonkin. We slept in Laotian *salas* or on the banks of the Mekong River. We went through those typically Laotian glade forests that were beautiful and peaceful as the very Laotians who crossed the roads, doleful yet carefree and full of the joy of living, and slow as the low-water Mekong itself.

My father was still the same violent and brutal character, but when he talked to me, his jet-black eyes became tender. His hesitant tenderness would take the form of a brusque, awkward caress, after which he would be back to shooting his mouth off in a tone to make the coolies and sentries blanch.

Being nonviolent, I got to adore that calm, peaceful country, the saffron-robed Buddhist monks surrounded by their entourage of novices with shaven heads, waving huge yellow paper parasols, their heavy alms bags slung around them; the Laotian women with their brightly-colored *sampoths,* their smooth round shoulders as if cast in bronze, their ever-present laughter, the flowers behind their ears. Unconsciously, I was in love with them because they were more womanly, more feline, more full-blown, and more buxom than the high-voiced, chattering women of Vietnam.

Laos was the Tahiti of Asia. Poor Tahiti, poor Asia . . . My wonderful country, my poor ravaged country, pillaged for thirty years. Country of my childhood that I will doubtless never see again . . .

By now, I had left the Couvent des Oiseaux in Dalat for the one in Hanoi. But only very briefly. The Americans bombed Hanoi. Three days of terror and cataclysm. The awful buzz coming nearer, nearer, and the muffled, swelling explosions, cellar walls shaking, hands over ears, heads between knees: "This one has our number on it," the breath of death passing us by, going beyond, the sound moving off and becoming the purr of a huge cat, the shiver I still feel today when I hear the howl of sirens. All the Hanoi lycées were evacuated.

I ended up with friends of my parents', druggists, in Hué, the capital of Annàm, for my last school year at the coed lycée. For the first time since the seventh grade, I was competing with boys again. I was furious when one of them got ahead of me, although that didn't happen too often; I remained among the leaders.

Naturally, I was still interested only in girls. After Renée, the daughter of the local *Résident*, who was superbly beautiful and dumb, there was Hélène, whose policeman father was head of the *Sûreté*. Pretty, a bit hefty, but funny and full of life. We were inseparable. We walked each other home and home again hours on end. We went sailing on the River of Perfumes, and we went on long bike rides to the Tombs of the Kings, the magnificent mausoleum-pagodas of the Imperial City. In school, of course, we sat side by side, and when her forearm grazed mine my heart skipped a beat at feeling her warmth so close to me.

We would write each other, too, of course, but it never occurred to me that I was experiencing anything other than friendship. Love, I believed, according to the books, was something that could be felt only for someone of the opposite sex. So these glows, these heartbeats, the sufferings and joys I felt could be nothing but friendship. Physically? As far as that was concerned, I was a real dope. There were times when I felt aroused, nervous, but I was quite unaware of the existence of masturbation. So I twisted panting in my bed, not knowing how nor being able to relieve myself. In any event, I threw myself wholeheartedly into my studies, and between them and my passionate friendships, life was truly full and such crises were rare.

The night of March 9, 1945, the Japanese attacked all the cities of Indochina and took power. I was just reviewing my history composition for the next day when, at 10 P.M., there was a cannon shot, then another, and another, and at last a general barrage. The pharmacist and his wife and I went down to the underground shelter they had had dug. We stayed there all night with the native boy and the *thi-haï*. We knew the battle was between the French forces billeted in the citadel and the Japanese who were storming it. But was it just a local skirmish or a general attack?

At dawn, the gunfire dwindled, and then it died away completely. We went after news. The garrison had surrendered. Everywhere in Indochina, arms had been laid down. I biked right over to Hélène's. Together we went to the hospital, to see whether we could be of any help. We were welcomed with open arms. The doctors were swamped, French and Japanese wounded lay everywhere on stretchers, and the few religious sisters could not cope with the work. As for the ladies of the Red Cross, so adept at organizing bazaars and parties, they were nowhere to be seen.

I spent eight incredible days there. I was constantly at the hospital, in my white smock and red-crossed armband with Japanese lettering that served as a pass. In the operating room, I saw arms and legs amputated, bullets extracted from gaping wounds. The wounded were tended without racial distinction, in order of seriousness. There was only one Japanese physician, who motionlessly watched the operations, taking notes, letting the French surgeons operate.

I was not quite sixteen yet. I remember the extraordinary feeling I had after my first round of night duty during which, by myself, I had taken care of fifty wounded, mopping their brows, giving them drinks, holding their hands.

Dawn was breaking, milky white; it was still rather cool, the hospital was silent. I had been in charge of the whole pavilion, alone, watching over it as it slept.

I looked out the window. The streets were deserted, a pedicab went slowly by, ghostlike, on the other side of the municipal park, and for one instant, drunk with joy and pride, I felt that I had watched over the sleep of the entire city.

At the end of a week, the Japanese requisitioned all cars, bicycles, radios, and weapons. They locked us in our villas, forbidding us to go out.

The French people of the whole region had been evacuated and brought in to Hué. They were piled in with us. All the houses were filled to overflowing.

Mother, her husband, and my little brother came in, each with one valise. The rest of their worldly goods lost for good . . .

There were now twelve of us in the villa. Every room was

occupied, except the dining room. It was the same everywhere; we were being introduced to the joys of overcrowding and collectivism.

We were cooped up that way in our shells for a month. The servants did the marketing and were able to set up communications between houses. I didn't see Hélène any more. Our homes were rather far apart but in between there were only stretches of rice paddies. I sent her messages by the native boys, and we signaled to each other from our windows. One day, I couldn't take it anymore. During siesta, I put on the *thi-haï*'s clothes, and her big conical hat, jumped the fence and scooted over to Hélène's through the rice paddies, walking along the little waterbreaks. That way, I was able to spend an hour talking to her and get back home before the grown-ups woke up.

I repeated this escapade two or three times at the risk of being shot at like a rabbit; for an hour with Hélène, I was ready to risk just about anything . . .

This was the time she chose to fall in love with the Japanese consul's son. He was very handsome, had a French mother, and of course was free to come and go at will. He called on her almost every day. I was consumed with hatred and fury. Hélène with a sweetheart, and a Jap at that! To try to divert myself, I started keeping a diary that I hid under a wardrobe—for there were searches carried out all the time, day and night.

Finally, after about a month, we were allowed out, within a certain fixed perimeter.

For thirteen months we lived that way, without a radio. The news came by way of a few Vietnamese who had remained friendly, and that news quickly grew wings and flew off to become wild rumors that we didn't really believe but endlessly passed on for the fun of it.

We knew we were at the end of the earth. The handful of whites in Asia were of no concern to anyone. The war wasn't over yet in Europe. After V-E Day, we began to wait and hope. De Gaulle and Leclerc must soon be going to launch a fleet, and bring an army to free the hundred thousand or so Frenchmen of Indochina, *n'est-ce pas?*

We expected an American landing at Tourane (Da Nang) any minute, or a parachute drop on Hué itself. Every evening, the spirits that we consulted in séances through our magic tables gave us "dates certain." The predictions would spread from villa to villa, and on those dates we would go to bed with our clothes on, ready for anything, sleeping lightly, briefly, hearts aflutter and hoping against hope.

Other nights, there were the tom-toms beating in the native city, beyond the River of Perfumes, and all around our concentration zone. Screaming squads of Viet Minh invaded the zone, paraded by, shouting threats, insults, political slogans, waving spears, machetes, rifles. The Japanese gave them their head, as was only natural, since they were the ones who had brought back Ho Chi Minh with them. They were helping the Vietnamese take their first steps into independence.

As for us, we went barefoot to market, for during the rainy season we wanted to spare what footwear we had left. The men got into the traces of a cart and the women and children pushed. We were allowed to go to market one day per week, and we had to stock up on supplies for twelve people. We waded through the mud, wearing latania-leaf rain capes and conical hats, like the Vietnamese.

The kids in the streets were the worst. They attacked us in gangs, armed with rocks and pebbles. They insulted us, hit us, knocked the carts over, and ran away laughing.

Engineers, professors, company managers, *Résidents,* picked up their provisions, got back into the harness in front of the cart, and were off again, weeping with rage, boiling with shame.

Since we had no more weapons, we made bamboo pikes, with beveled tips hardened in fire. Young men with these arms formed a kind of civil guard that warded off the hordes of street urchins along the road to the market. But at night, when the tom-toms beat, we could only wait in terror for a general onslaught. Each villa had its defense plan, its fall-back positions. Three of the villas were actually stormed, and two people were killed while three were abducted. One utility-company manager was sawed in half between two boards, and one merchant was found disemboweled, his genitals sewed into his mouth.

There was a cholera epidemic. But that, we were used to seeing. We, of course, were all vaccinated. But to see a coolie suddenly teeter as if drunk, collapse to the ground, and start to spew out his insides while his bowels were loosed, was something familiar to any child of the colonies, something we had always been used to having with us. Death was right beside you there in the street. But until now, it had never affected us whites. Now, it was different. At the Redemptorist Fathers' orphanage, two little boys had died. We drank all the rum we could get our hands on. Very good against cholera, everyone said. That was how I got soused the very first time.

As for school, well, I was finishing high school, but we were forbidden to attend. Organized courses sprang up, with volunteer teachers replacing our Vietnamese professors. A physician taught us science, an engineer mathematics. Classes were held almost anyplace, whatever might be available. We had to skip classes on market day, or cooking day, or because there was a riot or an air-raid alert; American planes flew over constantly. Sometimes they came skimming the rooftops, dipping their wings to buzz us and drop cases of medicines, which the "Viets" scooped up, with Japanese approval. Sometimes they dived and machinegunned us. Their behavior was rather unpredictable, but in the end, whether hostile or friendly, their presence did us good, reminding us that we were not abandoned, alone in a sea of hostile Asiatics, hunted down, cordoned off, isolated from the rest of the world.

One day, the Japanese decreed that a convoy of one hundred persons would be organized, to go and help build a road in Cochin China. Five kilograms [eleven pounds] of baggage were allowed. Our family was selected to be part of the convoy, to go off on foot and march over a thousand kilometers [six hundred miles] through the jungles of Annam and the mud of Cochin China. My brother was eight; I was sixteen. Hélène was not going along. We were desperate. Her Japanese sweetheart had been sent to Tonkin, and once again she could be all mine.

Two days before we were to leave, the Bomb changed all that. We stayed at Hué.

So don't anyone ever talk to me about guilt over Hiroshima. If it weren't for Hiroshima, I would have died on the roads of Indochina, the way those thousands of British did on the Burmese railway. Thanks to Hiroshima, I'm alive, I can shout, and sing, and love. I owe my life to Hiroshima. What to the rest of the world was a genocide that still plagues their consciences, for a handful of us was salvation. Without it, deep in the Cochin Chinese rice paddies, in the mudlands of the Mekong Delta, we would have perished of dysentery, of malaria, of beatings. Thank you, Hiroshima!

So, on August 17, we drank the last bottle of champagne, singing all the patriotic songs we could think of, beating time on our glasses with our forks. The war was over. In a few days, we would be free. We would go home to France.

Alas—the days went by, and nothing happened. The Japanese were still in charge and the Viets were getting wilder and wilder, more and more threatening. But we had been able to get back a radio, and that was now our big Sunday pastime. During the week we didn't have time to listen to the news, so a team of volunteers ran off a kind of mimeographed news sheet. But wild rumors had not ceased because of that. Now that they had some basis in actual fact, they were even harder to see through.

We were finally "liberated"—but by the Chinese, who were like an army of grasshoppers, gaunt and ragged, falling to on anything the Japs had left behind. Dazed Yunnan peasants who had never seen a bike now learned to ride one, zigzagging along the sidewalks. Standoffish officers were superbly gotten up in comic-opera uniforms. A colonel invited us to tea several times in the room he had requisitioned in a villa. He spoke a little English and behaved with perfect propriety. But when he asked Hélène and her sister and me all to become his wives at the same time, we never went back again.

On March 29, 1946, the French finally arrived, more than a year after our incarceration. We enjoyed our liberation, and celebrated it with as much joy and enthusiasm as the French in France had done. When I see pictures of the liberation of Paris, with the groups of children and women sitting up on the tanks, the flowers, the kisses, I think I am reliving our own great day. There were only five thousand of us, but some of the Leclerc Division soldiers who had "been in on" Paris told us that our welcome was even more overwhelming than that.

We were the lost children at the ends of the earth, and that night, at last, we could go to sleep in peace, not worrying about massacres or about armed robbery. We were once again in a little part of France and the sentry guarding the street corner was French, just like the rest of us.

Two days later, which happened to be my birthday, I attended my first real "party" at Hélène's parents'. Their guests were some handsome young cavalry officers, charming and nice. They taught us how to do the "swing," a dance that was new to us. They hummed all kinds of new French and American tunes like "Symphonie" and "In the Mood." Soon we had each paired off with one of the young men: mine was named Bernard Philiponnat. He was pink, small, and blond, pretty as a girl. He danced cheek to cheek with me, came to pick me up in his jeep, saw me home, and was just perfect.

Back at the villa, the adults started kidding me a little about my "boy friend." I flew into a rage. "No, he never even kissed me, and he won't kiss me. He's very proper. I don't even have to fend him off, because he doesn't try anything!"

When he left for Cochin China, I had no reason to grieve over losing my dancing partner.

My love was still all for Hélène. As soon as the Chinese came in, we had both taken the first of our final *baccalauréat* exams. There was an American outfit that brought the official examination papers up from Saigon. Another took them back down a week later, and we got the results by radio, one evening at ten, when personal messages were broadcast, for by now we had radio communications with the French at Saigon.

Since it was after curfew, the names of those who had passed were called out from villa to villa, along the streets and over the rice paddies. Dogs started to yelp and the little Chinese soldiers began running through our zone, wondering what had gotten into these whites who usually were so peaceful.

Two months later, we took the second part, which we had boned up for as best we could in the previous six months.

The groups of Americans who came through condescended to act as our intermediaries only in a very few instances. We had awaited them so enthusiastically that we were quick to be disillusioned. In their eyes, we were some kind of slavers, colonialists, collaborators with the Japanese, and they were all for the Viet Minh. The packages of medicines and powdered milk they brought went right across the River of Perfumes, to the Viets. The Americans were barely willing to listen to us, and my stepfather was hard put to get them to accept the dog tags of an American sergeant who had died during a forced landing in the bush. The other eight men in his outfit had been saved and hidden by my stepfather and his resistance contacts, and safely returned to a submarine in Quinh Non Bay. An unimpressed lieutenant took the dog tags, finally, but the sulfa drugs still went to the people across the river . . .

In August, we were finally able to leave Hué in military

trucks. A convoy of five hundred people headed for the Col des Nuages and Tourane (Da Nang). The first convoy had left a month earlier and I had received a letter from a girl I knew who was on it. She wrote, "When we had crossed the last pass and saw that all-white hospital ship waiting for us, we started to cry out with joy."

When we came down from the last pass in our turn, we saw a sooty old black boat. It was a coaler—with holds that had been more or less cleaned up so as to serve as a troopship. There was one water outlet on deck for five hundred people, and the latrines were roofless board structures.

For a week we lived like that, subsisting only on canned American army rations. The heat in the hold was torrid. Hélène and I slept on deck. We had staged a show on board, so we got to meet the officers, and were able to take showers, and sometimes to have lunch in their wardroom. The first lieutenant took a shine to me. I let him hold my hand in the moonlight, with Hélène along, because it meant some creature comforts for both of us. He was stupid, got on my nerves terribly, and once we got to Saigon I went out with him twice and then dropped him. My little lieutenant of dragoons Bernard Philiponnat was there now, and we went to Cholon to dance at the Grand Monde, had superb dinners in the Rue Catinat with cherry tarts and real French Camembert; in a word, we were living it up . . .

While waiting for repatriation, we stayed with my uncle, who was head doctor at the Cantho Hospital.

Since my days spent doing hospital work in March 1945, I had firmly decided to study medicine. In order to discourage me (as I was to learn only later), my uncle took me with him each day and had me tag after him on his rounds. For two months, in white smock and white cap, I was present again at operations, deliveries, the checkups of licensed prostitutes and of lepers. I was in heaven. I felt completely in my element. But my mother, in agreement with my uncle, decided that that was no profession for a woman. I would study law, then go on to the Poli-Sci School and the National School for Government Administrators.

No one asked me my opinion . . .

My father was dead.

My father had been massacred at Thakhek along with all the other men of the city. They had been taken away in trucks, through the beautiful Laotian glade forest. They had been made to dig a big trench, then had been cut down with bayonets and covered with quicklime. While we were sequestered, I had had no word from him. The wildest rumors had been rife. I kept repeating to myself, "If God exists, Papa is still alive. Dear God, I beg you, if you exist, give Papa back to me."

He was dead. An official Red Cross notice informed me of it in June. I went into our bedroom, closed my eyes, and said, "God, you don't exist. Now I know that. It's all over." To me the existence of God ended that day and forever. God died along with my father.

I burst into tears, I cried for an hour. I cried all of my grief out and went back to living. Three days later, I was dancing. I was seventeen, we were liberated, I was alive, and dancing was living. Crying would not bring Papa back. For a long time, I thought that maybe he had not died, that he had miraculously escaped the massacre and, wounded, having lost his memory, had been taken in by Laotian villagers and was still alive, hidden, at the end of the world, far from me, but alive. Henri Colpi's movie *So Long an Absence* affected me deeply, because its story was like that of my own wild hope.

But with the years, my dream turns more and more hopeless. Papa by now would be seventy-seven. Pretty soon I will have to bury him.

In March 1971, I was beside the Atlas swimming pool in Agadir with Aimée. I was reading a book by Jean Lartéguy, *Tambours de bronze* (Drums of Bronze). Suddenly I let out a yell that made her jump. I had just read the end: the Thakhek massacre had been engineered by a major just returned from

Burma, where the real thugs of the Japanese army had been sent. He had disappeared after that deliberate massacre and his country's surrender. Captured by a group of Thai partisans, he in turn had been executed a few months later.

It had taken me twenty-five years to find out my father had been avenged. He had died like a dog, with no grave of his own nor any cross to mark it, and there was I, getting a suntan at Agadir . . .

CHAPTER

II

We left Indochina on September 1, 1946, on the *Île-de-France*, which had been turned into a troop transport during the war and now, along with the *Pasteur*, was repatriating the Indochina French.

There were five thousand of us on board. Military and civilians. Women and children in cabins sleeping fifteen each. Water two hours a day for cleaning up. Standing in line for dinner and lunch, served by French waiters whom I addressed as "Monsieur," in my awe of them, since the only servants I had ever seen had all been Vietnamese.

I immediately got into the company that was setting up to stage a shipboard revue. A young military doctor was our director; in the troupe was a young women's auxiliary member called "Poussin" (Chick), who had interrupted her study of medicine to enlist as a nurse.

Since the women auxiliaries got the same treatment as the military, their food was disgusting. So I brought her packages of sandwiches that I left on her bunk. I noticed quite a few strange smiles on the lips of some of her cabinmates, but had no idea what they meant.

The revue was a hit. We repeated it the next night. By that time, we were already through the Suez Canal and past Port Said, in the Mediterranean.

Two more days and we would be in *France*.

After the last performance, the major treated the whole company to a drink. Then, Poussin invited me to go up on deck for a breath of air before turning in. I was delighted. It was beastly hot below decks where we had performed and even in the officers' wardroom. We slipped under a lifeboat.

Sitting there in the moonlight, without even a handrail between us and the edge, we could see the water splitting and foaming twenty meters below. Poussin put her arm around my shoulders.

"Cold?" she asked.

"No . . . not really . . ."

I was embarrassed. I didn't like this kind of touching. I hardly liked any kind of touching. Silence. Then Poussin said, "Do you know there are women who feel toward other women the way most women feel toward men?"

"Yes, I know."

"What do you think of it?"

"It's disgusting."

"What would you do if I kissed you?"

"Oh, please, don't!"

I must have sounded like I meant it, because Poussin laughed and, taking her arm away, said, "I was only kidding."

"Let's go on in."

For just one instant, panicky, terrified, I had thought: if she kisses me, I'll jump in. I really did think that. I need only to close my eyes to see that foaming water beneath me again, as if it had happened yesterday.

Poussin walked me back to my cabin, I went to bed. The next day I had a temperature of 104° and a fine case of bronchial pneumonia. I never saw the landing in the Promised Land. I couldn't even look out the porthole at the France that I had looked forward to seeing for so long. I was taken ashore on a stretcher and driven by ambulance somewhere near Montbéliard, where my stepfather had a sister who was married to the head of a large paper mill.

I discovered my charming twenty-year-old boy cousin, jazz,

and parties at the homes of the Peugeot and Japy families. I was learning about France, this wonderful country where you could walk around without worrying about being shot at, and everybody was French!

Happiness. Rebirth to a new life.

Yet we weren't wholeheartedly accepted. My little brother was taunted as "Chink" at the village school, and at the dances I was not considered a great catch. I must admit I made short work of any boy who tried dancing really "cheek to cheek" with me. I was not much fun. Nor was I especially pretty, flat as a Dover sole, all dark, with bobby sox and low heels, looking more the schoolmarm than the pussycat . . .

October was approaching. It had to be finally determined where I would study. My mother found me a room "with a local" in Paris and took me there before going back to Indochina with my little brother to rejoin my stepfather, busy as ever with his banks. My landlady was an ugly old thing who lived in a sixth-floor walkup, out behind the Latin Quarter near the Rue Monge Métro station. She was a real Wicked Witch of the West. A onetime cook, she spent all her time in her kitchen, griping to herself and cleaning her ovens with a vengeance. She occupied one of the bedrooms and rented me the other. A country-style boat-bed, dressing table topped by a washbowl with a jug of water, meticulously waxed floor shiny as a mirror, wallpaper with austere stripes, a smell of old age, ice-cold in that harsh winter of 1946—such was my new student home. My teeth chattered desperately in my little room. When I couldn't take the cold any longer, I would flee to the kitchen. The old lady would watch me study while grumbling at me, full of bitterness and resentment against the whole world.

I stayed in as little as possible. I dragged around with other repatriated girls, in the cafés near the Law School of the Sorbonne. We froze together. With icy noses, red ears, freezing hands shoved deep into our pockets, we were learning what winter was like, and it was no fun. Far, far away, the rice paddies, the China Sea, and water buffaloes wallowing in the mud . . .

All I had to live on was my government scholarship. It was meager, barely enough to get by on. Mother could not send me much extra. We had lost everything and the war damages that were to be reimbursed would take twenty years to be paid.

Fortunately, about half a year later, Mother came back to France for a few weeks and came across an old friend from Indochina, one of Papa's boyhood friends. I called him Uncle, and he changed the course of my whole life.

Oh, he took the very best care of me! Bald, garrulous, erudite, he taught me an infinite number of things about Paris and its different neighborhoods, about politics, literature, movies, and sex. Oh, yes, especially sex! He had a bachelor apartment in the Rue de Dunkerque, and after the biweekly luncheons I had at his home with him and his charming stupid wife, he would take me there from time to time, if we didn't go to the Cinémathèque or visit a museum.

I would take off my skirt so as not to wrinkle it, he would take off his jacket for presumably the same reason, and we would lie down on the bed. I snuggled up next to him and he talked away at me: about everything, about nothing, he fed me his erudition as a bird feeds its young. A lot about sex, and about love, of which I knew not the foggiest. He taught me the thirty-six positions and the number of cubic centimeters of semen a man ejaculates. I took it all in—Montherlant's books and the spermatozoa—all with the same eagerness and the same serenity.

Sometimes, in the middle of a sentence, he would stop, saying with a martyred expression, "Wait, wait a minute, I'm having an erection."

He seemed to be in pain. And I, innocent and unconcerned, waited for it to pass.

He would also say to me, "Never tell your future husband about these afternoons and the way we spend them. He'll never believe you. He'll think we made love. So never tell about it."

I agreed, though inwardly amused at it. Making love with this nice bald old man, what a weird idea!

He introduced me to one of his nieces, Françoise. Soon we were "best friends." By then, I had finally moved out of the old witch's and was living "on campus" at the Cité Universitaire. I had a private room with a view on the parks of Gentilly. Françoise was only in her third year of high school, but she was much more mature than her chronological sixteen years. She had the squinched-up face of a little Pekinese, and was wildly attractive. She wore Guerlain's Jicky perfume, which I switched to, and today, twenty-eight years later, I'm still using it. I still have the teddy bear she gave me, that I squirted with her scent and burrowed my nose into, to fall asleep at night.

I used to pick her up when she got out of the Our Lady of Zion School, and walk her back to Avenue de l'Observatoire, where she lived, and we would talk for hours on end. As soon as we parted, we wrote each other long serious, world-shaking letters. Her mother was not quite sure she approved. This was all the funnier because it was a matter of record that the lady in question had an attraction to those of her own sex; in Hanoi, back in the thirties, her slacks and her boyishly short haircut had caused many a raised eyebrow. But now, settled down and the mother of several children, she barely tolerated me. Françoise had to "scale the wall" to get out of an evening and come dancing at the Cité or go to the movies with me. Naturally, our pure best-friends relationship entailed no physical contact whatever.

We often talked about "lesbians," because the fate of those poor creatures bothered us considerably, especially me, since Uncle had taken me up to Carroll's on the Montagne Sainte-Geneviève, and these abnormal women interested me enormously. I even started writing a "slice-of-life" novel about them. And at times, in spite of everything, I had a sneaking doubt. When I went to see a ballet or musical, or a play, often one of the actresses would fascinate me, I would want desperately to meet her, and died of not daring to go and wait for her at the stage door to say—to say what to her, I did not know.

I consulted Uncle about this.

"Do you think I'm a lesbian by any chance? Only women seem to interest me, never a fellow. That's not normal."

He reassured me: "It is normal. It's just a phase that all women go through. You'll see, one day soon you'll meet a boy who will . . ."—you know the line.

Nevertheless, here I was eighteen, and still as untouched as ever! When Uncle introduced me to his friends, he'd say, "I'd like you to meet my niece from Indochina. She's eighteen, in her second year of law, and has never kissed a boy."

Everyone oohed and aahed over my purity and virtue. It was beginning to give me a royal pain. I had had enough of being an object of ridicule! I picked out a handsome blond boy who looked like my little lieutenant of dragoons back in Hué. He was completing his doctorate in law and worked at the Banque de l'Indochine, for he too was one of the repatriates. I really tagged around after him. He finally gave in, and one summer evening in the gardens of the Cité Universitaire, on a bench, he kissed me. I panicked. I had seen *For Whom the Bell Tolls*, and the scene in which Ingrid Bergman says to Gary Cooper, "I don't know how to kiss . . . Where do the noses go?" had really hit home with me, because I had always wondered the same thing. When he went after my lips, I don't know what I did. So I had to explain to him, "You'll have to excuse me, because I've never kissed anyone before."

He was flabbergasted. I was eighteen, alone in Paris for over a year already—the whole thing seemed unbelievable.

So we kissed. I found it rather uninteresting. I must say, he didn't kiss very well. He slipped a little bit of his tongue into my mouth, and bingo! we stayed motionless like that for minutes on end. I was happy at last to have been deflowered if only at that end, and triumphantly announced it to Uncle. But anything beyond that, no sirree! Poor Jean, who was twenty-five or twenty-six, had to be satisfied for the two or three months we went together with running his hands over my shoulders. I never even let him touch my breasts. They were, it is true, so small that I was ashamed of them and I had put up in huge letters in my room a line from Baudelaire that comforted me a little: "One is closer to the heart when the chest is flat."

It was after this inane flirtation that I met Françoise, and once again I lost interest in boys.

I was beginning my third year of law, and the future looked pretty dark. My stepfather was out of work, because his cashier had gone over to the Viet Minh with a huge sum of money, and he had been held responsible and dismissed. Having returned to France, my mother, brother, and he were living in the country on a tiny pension. My scholarship was still no more than a grubstake, so there was no question of my going on to any of the higher institutes of learning.

My stepfather's brother was a director at the French Gas-works, and there was a possibility of getting me in there as a consulting engineer, while I continued work toward my doctorate in law. That dizzying prospect seemed to me a fate worse than death. I had made up my mind, when I had had to give up medicine, that I would study law but then go into the Cours Simon to study acting. I felt that I was Hermione, that I was Phaedra, that I was Montherlant's Dead Queen—and now they were trying to foil that vocation of mine too.

I had even selected the scene I would audition for René Simon: the role of the Infanta in the Montherlant play, and I had posted in boldface on my wall, alongside the Baudelaire line, two of her speeches to Inez, expressing what I felt in the very deepest part of myself: "I have never been able to understand how one can love a man. Of the ones I have been near, I have seen that almost all were vulgar, and all cowardly . . ."

And then, especially, this one: "If a man had made himself so ridiculous as to love me, I should have paid him so little attention that I would have no recollection of it."

Meanwhile, the poor little student lost in Paris had found a warmth and a welcome with Maria Mériko, who had already become an actress. She lived with her mother, a babushka from Soviet Georgia whose violence and generosity reminded me of my own grandmother.

Actors used to come to rehearse in their cellar, which was set up as a small theater, and afterward we would eat blinis and piroshki with the Russian taxi drivers and with Francis Lemarque, the composer. Babushka would have liked me to marry him, for she looked on him somewhat as her son and me as her granddaughter. But I had no use for Francis and his guitar; my admiration was all for Maria, her warm voice, and her as yet undiscovered talent. She was not beautiful, but her charm was such that I spent hours cuddled up to her, entranced by her presence, listening to the men sing the beautiful nostalgic songs about their country.

That was when I met Guy, as simply as that, on the sidewalk of Boulevard Jourdan, when I went up to him and asked if he knew which was the Cuban Building of the Cité. "I just happen to be going there myself," he said. It was dark, I caught sight of a dazzling smile, immense black eyes. At the Cuban Building, the friend I was going to see had not yet come home. Guy suggested that I wait in the parlor with him. I accepted. He was handsome, cultured, brilliant, and emphasized the points he made with his long delicate artist's hands. He was working on a thesis in literature, already had a doctorate in law, painted, was interested in jazz. His father was an industrialist in Marseille. In a word, he had everything going for him, as the saying goes, and the homely little poor girl from the colonies was flattered, then proud, that he should even give her a second look.

Françoise detested him right off the bat. She found him fatuous and unappealing.

She was jealous.

As she had flunked her *baccalauréat*, her mother decreed

that my influence was not good for her, and sent her to finish out the school year at the Lycée français in London. We were torn, separating tearfully, drowning in despair, hanging on to each other's eyes, yet without even shaking hands, since we had always so stressed our deep disgust with physical "contacts," which "could be left to the lesbians."

We wrote each other twice a day, from Christmas to Easter.

Obviously, I saw more of Guy, now that I was unoccupied, and with all the free time I had previously devoted to Françoise.

Guy was a fervent follower of Garry Davis, that poor visionary Citizen of the World, who had gone and torn up his passport in front of the United States Embassy.

Guy had created a high-sounding "International Cultural Committee" under the auspices of UNESCO, and I became his amanuensis. He had decided to stage a show of Black theater art at the Cité Universitaire. It was taking on some proportions, and between visits to UNESCO or various government ministries, I was carrying on with Guy. That is to say, I was allowing him intimacies that barely went beyond the limits I had set for my first boy friend, the young banker: head and neck, now including the ears as well.

At Easter, Françoise came home to visit. I waited for her, my heart aflutter, in a tearoom we often went to, for she had the sweet tooth of a cat. She seemed changed to me, somewhat distant. She told me a lot of meaningless trivialities, and that she was making out with a fellow, who was big and tall and all, and they were even sleeping together sort of, but not going all the way.

My Françoise had ceased to exist. That little girl with her passion for literature, politics, the theater, had become a simpering birdbrain, half adolescent, half vamp. I had been betrayed, expelled from her futile world full of boys' hands.

That evening I gave in to Guy and went up to his room. A few days later, I let him take me.

Emotion? None.

Sensation? Zero.

Impression? Vacant.

I was satisfied to be playing at the grown-ups' game, but disappointed to find it so wanting in excitement. A slight arousal, a bit of curiosity, but mainly the discomfort of hearing a man moan and cry out. It struck me as indecent. Yet Guy was tender and violent in turn, careful to try to give me the pleasure I simulated, in no way egotistical, very imaginative, ardently out to prove his virility to me through gymnastic sessions filled with acrobatics that were at times tiresome and, at any rate, always boring.

Often, Françoise and I, with our dancing partners—had talked about orgasm.

We asked them how they could tell when a woman was having one. Bernard, a student at the Arts and Crafts School, told us that the sign that could never be faked was that when it happened, her lips pulled back as in a wide gaping grin. Popaul, who was studying aeronautics, said she would cry out and scratch atrociously.

My reaction comprised no grin, no outcry, no scratching. I asked a girl friend at the Cité who had had several lovers, "When you come, what's it like?" She replied with several details I no longer recall, but I told her, "I don't feel a thing."

"Don't worry," she said. "It doesn't happen right away. Be patient."

Patient I was. Still, nothing but that irritating and ever so mildly arousing gymnastic bit.

But let's return to the performance that Guy was putting on with some thirty Senegalese, Dahomean, Guinean, and Cameroonian students. Among them, several future government ministers, including Sonar Senghor, with his troupe of *siccos.*

Called *Black Incantation*, the performance was a big hit. Radio, TV (still in its infancy in 1950), and a few press notices, but all superraves. We were bathed in satisfaction. Guy decided to commercialize this success by playing in a Paris theater in order to amass some funds for the future shows of his "International Cultural Committee."

While checking out the theaters, he was also planning a surrealist festival. This was in April. A wonderful spring. Guy had gotten his company signed by the Théâtre de l'Étoile. We were stone broke. His parents gave him a very slim allowance, and my scholarship along with his check had to cover taxis, phones, sets, and costumes, for we were supposed to deliver a fully equipped production.

Bertrand Castelli, a young decorator, was part of our crew. He had designed very fine settings and we were now building them. We slept at the theater, right on the floor, living on Camembert and *baguettes* of bread.

We were to open in September. Our dancers all had scholarships that they could live on, but now they were turning into prima donnas and would be satisfied with nothing but the best. As for Sonar Senghor, he had dropped out entirely.

The great daily paper *Le Figaro* had organized a gala at Deauville and we had been invited there to perform *Black Incantation* as a result of the favorable article Maurice Bessy had written about us. We went there by chartered bus one fine Saturday in August. The Aga Khan was in the audience. Guy decided he would try to get him to make us a small grant. The dancers went back on the bus that evening, but Guy, Castelli, two of the performers, and I stayed on in Deauville.

Since all the hotels were booked solid, the manager of the gambling casino, François André, let us sleep on the benches of the roulette room after it closed at 2 A.M.

Before that, since I was still under age, he escorted me through the gaming rooms, explaining to me the intricacies of baccarat and roulette. I was fascinated as I watched the hundred-thousand-franc chips change hands. A whole stream of multicolored chips casually thrown on the tables!

It struck me how broke we were, just for trying to create something fine, and how a few of those uselessly wasted chips might account for a ballet, a show, a privileged moment. I was revolted; life was just too stupid.

The next morning, awakened early by the cleaning women, we whiled away the time until we could meet the Aga Khan. He was charming, and gave us a hundred thousand francs [at the time, about two hundred dollars].

We returned to Paris walking on air. This money would pay for the sets and part of the costumes. But that was not the way the dancers felt. After hours of endless discussion, they demanded that the money be split among them. They each got ten dollars or so, which they promptly spent, and we went back to looking for a subsidy and eating our Camembert.

September finally came. The dress rehearsal at the Étoile went off very well. Again, excellent notices. But we were only the first half of the bill that starred the old-time *chanteuse réaliste* Damia. Comebacks and nostalgia were not yet in vogue with theatergoers, so there never was a more bastardized split bill. Our own audience at the time—before the popularity of folk music and authenticity—was made up entirely of intellectuals and young people; the only ones who came to hear Damia were seventy-year-old domestics and concierges. The house was in an uproar every night, with the old biddies hissing our first part and the students getting up and walking out the minute Damia began intoning her standard tearjerkers.

In a word, fiasco. The manager refused to pay us the agreed-upon fees. We were bankrupt. We had left the Cité Universitaire, for I had given up studying law and Guy stopped preparing for his higher teaching degree. We had a room in a sordid little hotel near the theater and were living on fried eggs or pasta that I prepared on a hotplate.

Guy rebuilt the show. Departing from pure folk and giving it a unifying theme, he tried to turn it into a kind of African musical comedy. For a second act, he added some Caribbean numbers and bop dancers of the kind who were appearing in every Saint-Germain-des-Prés joint, in the hope of making it more "commercial."

The manager of the Théâtre Édouard-VII had taken us on, at the urging of Maurice Garçon, who had liked the show at the Étoile. We rehearsed in the theater foyer and he was setting up a tour to Madrid for us.

Just then Bertrand Castelli decided to organize his own company with a few deserters from ours, and he left for Italy with "his" sets.

Finally our *Ballets Nègres* show was ready for a more general audience. We had a tryout in the northern city of Roubaix. It went all right, although the house was half empty because it was an intolerably cold winter evening.

It was now January. And, oh, yes! In the meantime, I had become the star of the show!

Guy had finally had enough of his performers' blackmail every time they thought they had become indispensable, enough of their "Guy, I'm not going on tonight unless you give me a five-thousand-franc raise," and decided that the star had to be someone he could count on. He couldn't take on the job himself, because he couldn't sing a single note on key. So it was up to me.

I learned all the African songs by ear, filling in with a reasonable facsimile of the words, and Guy joined in for the dancing routines. I rehearsed on the stage of the Édouard-VII, in the set for the French production of *A Streetcar Named Desire*. I had to block out my movements between the bed, the table, chairs, rocker, and other assorted props, but finally one day I stepped out in the middle of the whole company. Everyone was amazed, but no one had any complaints.

To look the part, I darkened my complexion every night,

and in the program notes my mother became Chinese and my father Cuban—to justify my presence and explain my not looking so very Negroid.

And we were off to Spain. There were thirty in the company, twenty men and ten girls, plus a wardrobe woman, a nice little thing from Brittany named Maryvonne, who had been the chambermaid at our hotel until we led her down the primrose path. Now she was discovering the theater with its mysteries—and blacks with their big dicks—all at once. And she was beside herself.

There was one other white girl in the troupe, whom Guy had hired as a bop dancer. She was named Geneviève and was blonde, beautiful, and bursting with life and joy.

I liked her right away, but didn't feel passionately about her the way I had felt about Françoise. We still corresponded, but Françoise disapproved more and more of my way of life. She found Guy increasingly unacceptable as time went by. But he and I were now planning to get married, just as soon as we could get together the necessary legal documents.

He had proposed to me very early, even before that first show we staged at the Cité Universitaire.

I was a success!

For, to tell the truth, from the moment I had become his mistress, I had had only one goal: to get him to marry me. My pride and my honor demanded it. Where all his other girls had failed—since he was so resolutely opposed to the bonds of marriage—I wanted to succeed. Françoise sneered at me, saying I'd never make him do it. But I disagreed. I acted sweet and submissive, gaping with admiration for him. I repressed my fits of impatience, my violent rages, and got him to drop his guard and finally I nailed him. I had won my bet, and was more than a little proud of it.

He was very much in love with me. And when he took me in his arms and said, "I love you," I answered, "Me, too," and meant it—meant it, because of course love was something one could feel only for a person of the opposite sex.

So the tenderness I felt for him just had to be love. He was so nice, so attentive, so gallant—and so insatiable. Oh, insatiable, indeed! Despite all the upsetting problems that we were going through, he made love to me just as often and I was still awaiting that revelation of rapture.

So we got to Madrid.

Our show, at the Albeniz Theater, had the same fate as in Paris: hailed by the critics, but abandoned by the public. Even more at a loss than the French, the Spanish, who for the past ten years through civil and world wars had been isolated from the rest of the Western world, could not appreciate this rather special kind of performance. To them, the gyrating Negroes were nothing but shouting savages.

With our Albeniz contract finished, we stayed on in Spain, while Guy tried to set up a tour of the provinces.

We had moved to a *pension;* the luxury hotel we had been staying at now was beyond our means.

Geneviève was at another *pension*, with the rest of the troupe.

But we spent our days together, laughing, walking, sunbathing on the balcony of our room in Plaza Castellana.

And then, one night, I dreamt of her. I was holding her in my arms, kissing her on the mouth, and all over her golden blond body, and when my lips came to rest on her vagina, I awoke with a start. I sat up in bed, my throat dry, my heart palpitating. Guy, alongside me, was asleep, poor fellow. Beside him, the woman he loved and had married had ceased to exist. So this was it! Now I knew. This wonderful, amazing dream that had just swooshed through my guts and my heart was my Road to Damascus. Wiped out, dazzled, converted am I.

Saint Paul of Sex, Our Lady of Sappho, holy lesbian, pray for me. Open your arms to me. I have been born to the world of Love.

My eyes could now see those flaming "friendships" of my

childhood and adolescence, my surges toward women, my reluctance toward men, for what they were. Eyes wide open in the soft night of a Madrid springtime, I now understood why I had wanted to write that novel about the "poor lesbians," why I had been thrilled by Carroll's or the Monocle, where Uncle had taken me several times. What I had considered to be an entomologist's curiosity was really the call of nature, the call of my true life. "I'm a lesbian," I kept saying to myself. I was relieved, happy. I felt light. All the fog blew away, all veils were rent. I understood it all, discovered the true Elula, moved into my real skin, and I liked what I found—I liked it very much.

The next morning, Guy never suspected that overnight his wife had been translated.

Nor did I tell him. Now I had only one thing on my mind: I was in love with Geneviève, and now I knew it and had a wild desire to make love with her, to make the fabulous dream that had crashed through my horizon come true.

But how? I was a guileless child, my experience of *amour* nonexistent.

What did two women in love actually do when they got together in bed? Perhaps there were rites I was unaware of. I had no idea. No idea of how to go about even telling Geneviève that I loved her. I settled for silently adoring her, hating the men who surrounded and desired her.

Thereupon, we left Madrid for a tour in the Valencia and Alicante region. But we couldn't afford to take the whole company. We split up, and Geneviève with some ten of the blacks returned to Paris. Maryvonne, our nice little chambermaid, left too: she was pregnant, and needed to get an abortion as soon as possible, because a little black baby would hardly have been welcomed by her Breton family.

I remained alone with Guy and my sorrow. Geneviève was gone. My love had left me. I was a lesbian, yes, but with whom? For whom?

Guy went on making love to me, and I went on feeling

nothing. However, one night when we were at Valencia, and he was tenderly performing cunnilingus on me, something I rarely allowed because I didn't like him to do it—I was ashamed, it bothered me—an image suddenly appeared to me. I imagined he was I and I was Geneviève. I moaned, and almost, almost had an orgasm. But at the last moment I again bumped up against that closed impenetrable door: It was only he, it was only I . . .

More than ever, I wanted to make love with Geneviève. I was still writing to Françoise, and now I told her what was happening to me. She answered with an angry letter that compared me to Colette's Claudine at school, and told me that since I had now found my female mate, I was welcome to her—goodbye, and good riddance.

I never tried to see her again. She is now married to a tenured high government official, has three kids, and is probably a stinking society lady who cheats on her husband with his young underlings.

During my emotional moulting, we had gone southward through Spain, from flop to fiasco, passed over the Straits, and ended up in Casablanca, where Guy had gotten us a booking.

The show did not go over any better there. And, anyway, we were just the ghost of the company we had been. The thirty we had been at first had now dwindled to fewer than a dozen. It was no longer a show of much substance, even for the nightclub in which we were appearing, on the cliffside road at Ain Diab. The management refused to pay us, and Guy had to do what he had always tried to avoid: appeal for help from daddy's business in Marseille. His father sent enough for the repatriation of the few remaining members of the cast, but Guy and I were left stranded in Casablanca.

What next? I found a job as a Cuban singer in a Russian nightclub, the Rora, also up on the cliffside road.

Yes, instead of a dancer, now I was a Cuban singer. This had come about earlier in Alicante. One evening when the house was rougher than usual and we were getting a bit scared backstage, Guy had said to me, "Go out there, and do whatever you want—but do it in Spanish!"

I went out, to a chorus of hisses. We had been in Spain for a couple of months, and I was beginning to pick up a nice line of broken Spanish. So I said, *"Buenas tardes. Yo voy a cantar una canción para ustedes."*

And I barged valiantly into *el tuba del momento*, without any accompaniment whatsoever: "Dark Angels," which the radio played a zillion times a day.

They raised the roof. It was a sensation! The Spaniards were so delighted even to hear something hummed in their own language after an hour of barbaric chanting that they yipped and yelled.

Immediately, a new section was added to our production, in the second half of the show, during the Caribbean numbers: a group of songs on tom-toms and bongos, the only musical accompaniment we had. It helped us avoid too many tomatoes.

I sang badly. Not quite on key, but not really off key, with a thin little voice, no, to be honest, a whisper, but I succeeded in doing it with some grace and charm. People "watched" me sing rather than listened to me, and that was better. Lascivious, sensual, I waved and wiggled, really lived the boleros and sambas that made up my repertoire, and the audiences loved it!

So I sang on for three months at that Russian cabaret. Ever since, I've become sick at the mere sound of gypsy music, that's how bad the band was that I had to put up with every night. "Ochi chorniya" makes me ill, "Kalinka" turns my stomach, and in Paris I've never set foot inside the Raspoutine, Monseigneur, or other Russian night spots.

While I was at the Rora every night from ten to two, Guy —well, Guy wasn't doing anything. I would leave him in front of some blank paper, because he was trying to write a novel, and when I got back to our flea- and bedbug-infested hotel, the paper was still blank, but he was ready to make love to me.

I was losing patience; my whole being was revolting against both his idleness and the more and more unbearable rhythmic gymnastics. I could think only of Her. She was supposed to have come back to join us in Morocco, but now, after the breakup of the troupe, she was stranded in Paris. She wrote me nice amusing letters, never dreaming how I was burning up, dying for the taste of her lips, her blond belly, her golden shoulders, her tender neck . . .

Finally, after three months, by dint of living a spartan life, eating on the beach or at Arab restaurants in the Medina where flies came right down into the couscous, we had enough money put aside to take a lease on a little club in the center of the city, right next to Casablanca's music hall, the Tabarin.

Guy had decorated the club, which he named the Shango, in Afro-Cuban style, reminiscent of the sets for our ballets. Poor old sets! They had remained hostage to some unpaid innkeeper in Spain.

As you entered the club, on the right was the bar, then on each side, along the dance floor, little barrel-shaped low tables, with barrel-shaped stools. In the back, a painted drop depicting a jungle village, a path, some fetishes. To either side, in the corners, a little straw-roofed hut. In one were the piano and pianist, in the other, behind a multi-colored curtain, a tiny room in which I dressed and made myself ready for my singing sets.

It was charming, the naive paintings bursting with bright colors. I was twenty, young, fresh, gracious, and the West Indian combo of six we had brought from Paris was very good. In a word, we were an instant success. I acted as hostess and sang. All Morocco came to see me.

Guy staged my songs in a highly suggestive, sensuous way,

and whenever there was any kind of benefit I was always asked to appear and regularly made the front page of the local papers.

But what was my life like, in all of this?

To begin with, shortly before, we had finally gotten married, without any to-do, just the two requisite witnesses. No bouquets, no orange blossoms. A quick wedding, with neither honeymoon nor presents. The marriage that I had wanted and so masterfully plotted for no longer meant anything to me. I had put it off as long as possible. "We're just fine the way we are," I kept saying. But Guy kept insisting, and I finally gave in, mainly for the sake of my mother, who was not too happy at the idea that we were living together.

Poor Mother! What I put her through!

We had brought her to Casa to be the cashier and to tend bar at the Shango. Nothing daunted. Poor Maman, all five feet of her, looking like a purebred Asiatic and fifty years old, having to serve drinks and make small talk with the locals who came to town looking for action! We had no B-girls. We refused to. This was before the day of the discothèques, but we already tried to run that kind of club. People weren't accustomed to it, and the cruisers, the back-country folk in for a good time, the big spenders, were disappointed and did not come back.

I was beginning to find out what people were like. The bashful girl student, the wise virgin, had not turned into a courtesan despite appearances, and my naiveté still remained distressingly unimpaired.

One day, a Moroccan customer who was the spit and image of Dario Moréno and had just recently become a big shot in his country, asked Guy whether he might take me to visit his harem and meet his wives. Guy was guilelessly agreeable, and so was I. I was thrilled at the idea of seeing the inside of an Arab home—especially the harem part.

He comes by car to pick me up at the hotel about 3 P.M.

I'm made up and dressed to the nines. Ben X stops on a downtown street. Strange place, I think, for a harem. However . . .

"Coming in with me? I just have to stop off at my office for a minute, then we'll go on home."

Oh, well, in that case, it makes sense.

We go up six flights, and now I'm at a loss. He opens the door, and I see a studio bed, a little table, two glasses and a bottle of port wine. The classical assignation setup: clear enough.

Ben X tries to put his arms around me.

I don't know just how I went about it, what I may have said, with what kind of persuasiveness or diplomacy, but at any rate, an hour later Ben X was on his knees before me, kissing my hands, calling me his little sister, and swearing that if anyone ever were disrespectful to me, I had only to call and Zorro would come charging to the rescue!

Ben X took me straight back to the hotel without showing me his harem. The fact, of course, was that he didn't have one. He had only one wife, and she was a European.

Guy and I had a good laugh over this adventure, but the truth of it is that never in my life did a man really attack me, bother me, overwhelm me with phone calls or pressing demands for rendezvous. I know how to put them on such a plane right off that they subconsciously realize they'd do better not to try. For even men who are fatuous and pretentious are not necessarily incapable of understanding, and they can quickly tell whether there is a chink in the defense put up against them.

So, when some girl complains to me that she's been pestered by one or several men, I can never believe she is pure as the driven snow. In reality, that wooing, that pursuit, appeals to her, even if only for the pleasure of repulsing it. She wants or needs such "compliments" as proof. Proof of what? Of her beauty, her attractiveness?

I want those proofs, too, and I get them, from women, from The Woman, and that's enough for me, since She is the one I want to please, the one I want to love.

As for men, what I ask of them is comradeship, and a kind of complicity if they are intelligent, cultured, and delicate, and I can admire or respect them. Nothing else. And very quickly, the worthwhile ones respond. So I have good men friends, some of whom like me very much, as they would a little or a big sister, even if once in a while a touch of incest gets hold of them.

There were also women who were attentive to me, since I was the big attraction in town, whatever that meant. One of them, very beautiful and very blond, trapped me between doors, rubbed her well-endowed body against me, tried to bite my lips or my shoulders that were bare in my Cuban costumes, and suggested it might be fun to try three-way parties (with her husband) or foursomes (if Guy were willing to join us).

That didn't interest me. It revolted me. What I wanted was to find out how to make love with a woman who loved only women, so that later I might offer my body, my heart, and all my newly acquired know-how to Geneviève.

I set my sights on the barmaid of the Tabarin, the music hall right up from the Shango.

She was a lesbian, without any doubt. Tailored clothes, man's shirt, shoelace necktie, boyish haircut, a true caricature. And rather pretty, with big, very sweet black eyes. But that was not the main thing. The main thing was that I needed a teacher from whom I could get my first lesbian lesson, and there were only two "acknowledged lesbians" in all Casablanca: one was sixty years old, and the other, this barmaid, was thirty-two. So no question about it! She was the one for me.

I started doing my dance of the seven veils. Moustique (to cap it all, she was known as Moustique, or Mosquito!)

was a little slow in catching on. She couldn't believe her eyes. This eager young quail falling into her arms, coming on to her, forcing her to set up a date . . .

One afternoon at last I went to her. I left the hotel at two, saying I was going out to buy some books. A carriage took me to Rue de l'Horloge. I paid the driver and went into an ordinary lower-middle-class building. Moustique was waiting for me. She lived with her parents and with a four-year-old daughter she had had by a close friend. While the kid played in another room, we sat on the cheap mail-order sofa, talking about this and that. There were long silences. We knew very well what we had gotten together for.

Finally, Moustique moved closer and hugged me. She kissed me. Her lips were cool, soft, infinitely sweet, exciting in their mobility, compared to the hard, compact lips of men. Her tongue was tender, adept, and sweet as well. Such sweetnesses—I was submerged in the sweetness of this first kiss from a woman. We kissed at length, not saying a word. Nothing needed to be said. She stroked me softly, bashfully, still unable quite to believe her good fortune. I felt wonderful. I was melting . . .

But that was as far as we could go, with the kid coming in from time to time, and her parents likely to come home at any moment.

We made a date for the next day—same time—at a café on the Place de France.

The wait seemed endless to me. I rushed to join her with my heart going wild. She was waiting for me, sipping a mint tea. She took me to a nearby hotel, kept by an old dyke she knew. The bedroom door was barely closed when she started to kiss me again. At length. Then, suddenly releasing me, she said, "Get undressed." She did the same.

It hit me like an ice-cold shower. I was petrified. I almost turned and ran. I was not a whore, to strip like this, on command. I forced myself to stay, for Geneviève's sake. I had to know, I had to learn. But from that shock I have retained a kind of timidity, an infinite panic over that crucial moment when a mere flirtation turns into a love affair.

I am always apprehensive about that moment which can take all the poetry away, when in fact there is such beauty, such emotion in the slow approach of two bodies discovering one another, uncovering themselves, proceeding to their nudity, little by little, piece by piece.

That moment which can spoil it all or make it all more intoxicating, more exciting. The slow approach, the zipper slipping down, the button which, opening, lets a hand get through; the hooks that make way to fill your palm with the hot flesh of a breast, the warmth of a hip . . .

So I undressed and dove into the bed, stiff, tight. Moustique slipped in alongside me. Her little body was not very attractive, her breasts were tiny. I looked upon her without pleasure or emotion, the way you look at a new teacher the first day of school. She kissed me again and made love to me. And that was how I became a lesbian.

I catch my breath, close my eyes. I'm feeling just fine. But I have to go further. This unexpected discovery of fulfillment is a bonus from heaven.

The fact is, I am here to learn how to make love to the woman I love, Geneviève, my desire, my revelation. So I go over to the attack. In my turn now, I am on top of Moustique with her bleak neuter body, but her sex is a woman's. Since I am unacquainted with masturbation, my hand goes down hesitantly. I am afraid I won't know how, won't be able to find the spot, so sensitive, so small, so intense.

My lips will be better able, I think. I slide down along her body. My lips go down on her vulva. And all at once, I am in the forest, in the moss, I am the newborn babe, the prostrate worshiper, I am quenching my thirst at the spring after twenty years in the desert. I inhale, I drink, I roll about, roll myself in. Without knowing how, I do know. Gestures that have come from the depths of me because I am a woman and I feel and know what The Other Woman may want.

When at times I had wanted to make oral love to Guy, it had turned my stomach. That column pushing into my gullet was like shoving two fingers down my throat to make myself vomit.

And the odor of the sperm, so cloyingly sweet, nauseating, sticky . . .

Here, my tongue, my lips, my nostrils took in the taste and smell of moss and moist algae. I was reminded of Henry Miller and a hymn to the sex of woman which he compared to a grotto resounding with organ music as smooth as silk, endowed with marrowy recesses, eiderdowns, and mulberry leaves, and that which I had reread so many times, unconsciously turned on by it, now was bursting right into my head, on my tongue.

Moustique came. I was proud of myself.

She could hardly believe it was the first time I had made love to a woman. When I said, "Teach me," she murmured, "You have nothing to learn. Just do as I do." I obeyed. I was lucky. The teacher I had latched on to was sensational.

During the months that our affair lasted, Moustique taught me everything, showed me everything, made me feel everything. No other woman ever revealed anything further to me. At the first try, I had learned the whole scale. I had learned to play the great aria of love. Only the strings were to vary and make some of the tunes better than others.

As I left Moustique I was weak in the knees, drunk with joy and exaltation.

I went to see my mother and announced to her that I had just slept with a woman and was a lesbian. She raised her eyes heavenward and, with her Oriental fatalism, replied, "What can I tell you? If you are twisted, it's not your fault, I'm the one who made you . . ."

"I'm going to get a divorce."

"Why?"

"Because I can't tolerate making love with a man any more."

On this, she could not agree. Marriage was a social step upward, and was to be preserved. I promised her I'd think it over and not do anything rash. I merely ducked Guy's advances for two or three days. When we did have intercourse again, I found it completely unbearable. I knew now that I could vibrate in another way, at last, and his caresses were exasperating.

Two days after that, he found a letter from Moustique in my bag. Just a harmless, silly, conventional love letter, but it threw him for a loop.

I was having dinner at the Shango with Moustique. It was 9 P.M. Except for the little Moroccan waiter serving us, there was no one there yet.

Guy marched in, livid. Slimmer, paler than ever. His eyes, soft and tender like a monkey's or a spaniel's, were unrecognizable. He came down the three steps into the Shango, straight at us, raised his hand, and slapped Moustique.

"Out of here, bitch. Beat it! You're not going to take my wife away from me."

Moustique had stood up and, on her tiny high horse, tried to hit him wildly with her little fists. Then I got up. I separated them.

"Go ahead," I told her. "I'll see you later."

I was not afraid of Guy. He wasn't a battler. Once he had given her that smack, he stood stock-still, trembling.

"I don't want her in here ever again."

"Then I won't be here either."

"Are you sleeping with her?"

"Yes, I'm sleeping with her. And I won't, I can't be your wife anymore. Let's get a divorce."

"Never. There won't be any divorce."

It was a short argument. I laid my conditions down to an

emptied, docile man. We agreed, no divorce, since that was how he wanted it.

"I love you," he kept repeating.

Okay. I would go on living with him, but would see Moustique whenever I felt like it. At any rate, I wasn't going to live with her, I didn't love her. I was as if under a spell, thinking only of lovemaking, everywhere, all the time. We spent our afternoons at the old dyke's hotel; I came away with drooping eyes, empty-headed, spent, exhausted, concerned only with when we would meet again. I was neglecting the Shango. I even slipped out during the night, to make love some more, anyplace, in a hallway, in a car.

I had demanded that Moustique be allowed freely back into the Shango. But the tension between her and Guy did not let up. He thought she was ugly, stupid, and nasty. He was quite right. She was wildly in love with me and begging me to leave him. I promised whatever she wanted, not caring what it was: She made me come.

I was making up for my overly staid adolescence, making love for the sake of all that innocent child's "friendships."

And there's no point in saying, "That's normal: Like all lesbians, she must have been a clitoridean."

Wrong.

We are all anatomically the same, and therefore equal in our potential for orgasm. But everyone now knows at least the basic proposition, that climax has its seat in the head and not in the genitals.

What is less well known is that the vagina has nerve endings for only about the first two inches, and it is only along this ridiculously small distance that rubbing can produce a sensation and bring about an orgasm.

So—a super-phallus, or an average tool, or soft, skilled hands, what difference does it make?

What is a sure thing is that, while clitoral enjoyment is most often instinctual, vaginal enjoyment has to be learned.

It has to be mastered, it is rarely innate in a woman. So, since it has to be learned, it requires tenderness, patience, intuition. A strong, powerful drive into the bush is not enough. A two-ton truck is not the best vehicle for exploring little country lanes . . .

One of the greatest voluptuous sensations I know is that of initiating a woman into this sort of orgasm, when all she has known was men who possessed her without giving her the slightest tremor of real enjoyment.

People should get over imagining that love between two women is limited to a few little lip-and-tongue games. We are able to come with our entire bodies. Our enjoyment is not merely superficial, and no more than a mature heterosexual woman can we be satisfied merely with the "introductory trifles."

No, whether I was or wasn't vaginal was not what made me become a lesbian. Sex was still something new in my life, while in my heart women had ever and always reigned supreme.

My religious education—for at Than Hoa I had been a very fervent believer—had had indelible consequences. My loving friendships had always remained platonic. I remember how I had avoided physical contact, how I had caressed the long fragrant hair of Nicole and then hated her so for it that I had killed her trained mouse. Wasn't it because I was unconsciously fighting the emotion I was feeling for her? And what about Françoise, and our alleged revulsion against any contact? Was it not simply that I was fleeing women, for fear that I might reveal I loved them too well?

But now, how I was leaving behind that aversion to contact, how I was making up for all that I'd missed!

Business at the Shango suffered for it. The crowds had been coming to see that charming little singer in the club that had no hookers and maintained a certain class and tone. But now that young singer, whose picture continued to make page one of the Moroccan papers, was becoming more and more abrasive with men, baring her fangs if they so much as paid her a compliment, coming in late, disappearing unpredictably, and always seeming to be thinking of something else.

Soon my affair with Moustique was no secret, and "friends" began to urge Guy to do something about the scandalous carryings-on.

We were still in the same hotel room near the Shango. Guy had lost weight. All you could see on his face was his big sad dark eyes. When we got home at dawn, I would fall asleep dreaming of the afternoon ahead, and he stayed up, drawing me, painting me.

That was the only way he could still have me. He took me in my sleep, sketch after sketch, seizing furtive expressions, unplanned gestures. Sometimes I would awaken, and seeing him sitting on the edge of the bed that way, sketching me, made me uncomfortable, made it hard for me to go back to sleep. Once I called out in my sleep, "Leave my four hands free!"

As soon as I was up, I was off to be with Moustique at the old dyke's hotel and didn't leave there till it was time to go and have dinner at the Shango and then get ready for work. Business got worse and worse. Mother went back to Paris, because her husband felt she was a bit old to be playing barmaid in some joint halfway around the world.

We hired a Swiss girl who knew her business well and whom Guy slept with a little, taking a thousand precautions, although I couldn't have cared less.

One day, we had to face it: We were broke.

The Shango closed its doors. Guy packed and went back to Marseille to work for his father. There was no other way out. His dreams of painting, writing, directing, and producing shows had grown threadbare in Spain, then finally worn through at Casablanca. There was nothing left but the Marseille factories . . .

I stayed on a few days in Casa to satiate myself with love and complete my education. It was a beautiful way to end it!

Moustique took me out into the back country, where a friend had lent her his bungalow. Now, before leaving it, I saw the real Morocco.

What mastery, what passion, what energy, what imaginative wildness there was in this woman who was so primitively vulgar in everyday life! In bed, she became a Bacchante, a Prince Charming, a Marquis de Sade, a mad mistress, delicate page, whore and bitch.

The little girl I had still been when I met her now was prepared to love, to give, to receive. I had learned my lessons clearly and well, while my heart remained with Geneviève, and now I was impatient to bring her all the crazy, frenetic, wonderful things I had come to know with this little lesbian.

I finally departed Casablanca, leaving behind me a desperate lovesick and loveworn creature, but before joining Guy in Marseille, I made a detour by way of Paris.

By way of Paris, in order to see Geneviève once again!

CHAPTER

III

SHE LIVED ON PLACE FURSTENBERG.

I dashed up the four flights with my heart beating wildly. She was not alone. Yves C., her new boy friend, was with her.

He was ugly and had a limp, he beat her and was broke.

She was more beautiful, more striking, and blonder than ever. I was bursting with love, jealousy, hate.

She laughed when she heard of my new "sex preference." She thought it amusing. He made a face. We detested each other right off.

For a week, we played out a hellish triangle. We criss-crossed Paris in C.'s patched-up jalopy that got a bare ten miles to a gallon of water and had us stopping at every public water spout and fountain in town. I didn't want to leave Geneviève this way, but he was suspicious and jealous and was constantly with us.

After a week, I gave up and left for Marseille without having had the courage or opportunity to tell her that I loved her.

I was all mixed up. In Marseille, I found that Guy was equally at sea. We had bollixed up everything until now, our private lives as well as our public . . . We really ought to make an effort to start all over.

He picked me up at the railroad station, and we went right out to Le Lavandou to spend a weekend.

We had a nostalgic dinner, reminisced over the two wild

years we had had together, by mutual agreement not mentioning the last several months.

It was June. Our room had a view on the sea. There was moonlight, and there were pines, the sound of the waves, and the hurt of our two disappointed lives.

Guy took me in his arms. I huddled against him. He kissed me softly on the face, eyes, lips. I let him. He loved me, he had proved it. I could not hope for more thoughtful, dependable, or sincere companionship. There could only be affection, since my love for him had turned out to be hopeless.

When his tongue went after mine, I succeeded for a moment in warding off my disgust, but then I had to turn away. I just *could not.*

I was heartbroken about it, but nothing doing. Wordlessly, we lingered in each other's arms.

Then life, everyday life, resumed its course.

We never again referred to that moment at Le Lavandou. Never again did Guy make any effort to overcome or persuade me.

For several years, we were to sleep side by side in the same bed, without his ever losing his composure.

And I, still the selfish, thoughtless youngster, would parade around nude, and sleep nude next to him. The body that he still loved, the beauty he still must have desired, rubbed against him in sleep, snuggled up to him in the cold. And never once did he weaken. Never did he lose control. He loved me as no one has ever loved me: hoping for nothing, asking for nothing, getting nothing in return.

And I took it all perfectly for granted! He knew me well, knew that at the slightest suggestion I would have reared up, pulled back, and fled.

So we started our life in Marseille. The prodigal son had returned to the hearth, but no fatted calf had been killed for the occasion.

Guy got a ridiculously low salary, but we were provided with food and a roof over our heads.

His family were of almost Protestant severity and austerity. Very nice people, good company, but appallingly conformist, sodden with tradition.

So we had to act the happy little couple before his folks, but the minute we were alone in the apartment they had furnished for us in the large villa that the whole clan lived in, we carried on like maniacs, jumping around on the Louis XV furniture, skidding around on the Oriental rugs, and playing endless games of belote in our very unconjugal bed.

In August, Geneviève came down to Juan-les-Pins with some musician friends who were playing at the Vieux-Colombier.

We spent the weekend there with her.

Seeing her again, tanned, statuesque in her white swimsuit, her long blond hair caressing her caramel-colored shoulders, took my breath away.

In the evening, we listened to a bit of jazz, and then she wanted to turn in. We walked through the noisy crowd celebrating the feast of the Assumption, wordlessly, holding hands.

On the beach, I had told her—entirely in the past tense—how much I had been in love with her back in Spain. She had sighed, "Too bad I didn't know . . ."

Now here we were, just the two of us, in festive Juan-les-Pins, and I asked, "Can I see you up to your room?"

She acquiesced.

I undressed with a palpitating heart. This was the time to go into action. Now or never. My time had come. Here was my destiny . . . I was terrified. I didn't know what I would do, how I would ever dare.

I went into the bedroom. She had already turned out the light, and I did not turn it back on. I sat down on the bed. Long silence. If she hadn't put her hand on mine, I would probably have gotten up and left.

Then I found enough courage to bend over her face. The moment my lips touched hers was an eternity. I had been waiting for this for twenty-one and a half years. Her lips were hot and fleshy, her tongue knowledgeable, alive, an enveloping sweetness. Her blond hair mixed with my black, both equally long. Her breasts were like soft, snowy hillocks, her skin was smooth beneath my fingers.

My nails had grown long since Morocco. I impatiently bit them down, so as not to hurt her.

And then I made pitiful love to her—I didn't know how any more. I had forgotten all the right moves. I now had to reinvent the things I had learned just for her. Every time I've been really in love, I've had to reinvent lovemaking. To maneuver properly on the battlefield that is the bed of love, a girl has to have all her head about her, not her heart. Too much love, too much desire, can make a woman as impotent as a man.

So there was no unforgettable sexual summit—still I was happy, dazzled with happiness. Geneviève had accepted my love. She even told me that she loved me.

The next day she was off to Paris.

I could not forget her. I couldn't live away from her, without her, my love finally come true, my first love!

I decided to follow her. And since I had made a bit of a name for myself and gotten a little experience singing in Casablanca, I decided I would sing for my supper.

I had to break the news to Guy. I did it as nicely as possible.

He wept, "Go, you are free, but remember there is always a place for you here if one day you change your mind. And for the sake of my parents, so they won't be unhappy and won't know that you've left me, please just arrange to come back here from time to time."

I said yes to everything. I was no longer in Marseille by now but already *auprès de ma blonde* . . .

I left saying that I had to go and visit my mother. I was walking on air. Life was beginning!

But hardly had I arrived when it all fell in.

Despite all her promises, Geneviève was still shacked up with C., who was scurvier than ever, and Moustique, having heard I was in Paris, now arrived on the scene and started treating me to the big second-act showdown scene.

Since I could not live with Geneviève, on account of C., I stayed with Moustique. We made love again. But now, I just let her love me, completely passively. I had no desire for her skimpy neuter body. I merely let myself enjoy the pleasure she was able to afford me.

In the evening, when she went to work at Chez Moun, a "femme" nightclub in the Pigalle area where she was now a "hostess-waitress," I skipped out and across town to Place Furstenberg, to Geneviève's.

The studio she lived in was up beneath the roof and belonged to a nice old gentleman everyone called Tonton. He lived on the second floor in a strange and fascinating apartment.

He was a former governor from the French colonies and in his rooms, which had heavy dark drapes and rare Chinese art objects and valuable African masks, he always kept two or three young girls from the provinces, new to the fleshpots of Paris.

They paid for their keep by letting Tonton have a few harmless free feels. To see and hear the charming seventy-five-year-old man, refined and cultivated, his hands wandering suggestively over them, endlessly expound about the firmness of an ass or the curve of a tit, was a show in itself.

In order to avoid being surprised by C., Geneviève and I had our rendezvous at Tonton's. Since Geneviève always refused to turn off the lights, I think that perhaps from behind some picture or drapery Tonton may have had himself a few good voyeuristic times with us. I never did find out for sure. I only wondered about it much later. At that time, I was too young and naive even to conceive of anything like that—much less suspect that Geneviève might have been a party to his game. But, in all likelihood, she too needed to pay her rent.

I would dash away at top speed, just in time to catch the

last *métro*. In the train taking me up to Pigalle, where I shared a hotel room with Moustique, stockings and garters hastily stuffed into a pocket of my coat, eyes closed, lips puffy from our kisses, I was happy. I loved a woman and a woman loved me.

Despite this, I desperately needed work. In the meantime, we were living on the travel money Guy had given me when I left and what Moustique brought home from the cabaret. A real "hostess-waitress" or B-girl (not the kind who is expected to go home with the customers at the end of the night) earns her living at the cost of her health: for every champagne bottle uncorked, a little more money, a little more alcohol, and a little more drunkenness. Moustique came home polluted every morning. Besides, she was very ill and was vomiting blood.

She had brought her daughter up from Casablanca and all three of us lived together in the sordid room of a sordid hookers' hotel in Rue Pigalle. We were on the third floor, and when I got home from Geneviève's at 1 A.M. I would have to breast a steady stream of couples going up or coming down from the quick-turnover rooms on the second. The racket went on all night, and I carefully locked my door ever since a drunken G.I. had once busted in during the night.

Early in the morning, the hustle-bustle stopped. Then it was the musicians, dancers, and hostesses from the nearby *boîtes* coming home. By seven in the morning, the hotel was all quiet, and it stayed that way till twilight. But for us, this was the time to get the little one ready for school and take her there. Only after that, at about nine, could we finally get some sleep.

I simply had to find a way out of this filthy sowbug's life, hidden away from the light of day. So I looked for work. But there too I was in for a shock: Paris hadn't exactly been waiting for me.

At that time, 1951, there were none of the little Left Bank cabarets yet. To get a start as a singer, there was only the ABC, the one big legitimate vaudeville house, and the old-fashioned cabarets where, if you were breaking in, you were expected to "do the customers" when you'd finished your turn. I wasn't having any of that! But I wasn't really ready for the ABC yet either. Not even ready to ask for an audition.

I was offered a small part in what was described to me as a "pinup movie," but the casting director wanted to feel me up the way Tonton did with his fillies, so I decided the prudent course was to tell him, "Don't call me, I'll call you."

What did that leave? Well, the cabarets where I might feel a little safer, because I would be surrounded by women like myself, the ones like Carroll's or Suzy Solidor's. I certainly didn't want to have anything to do with the low femme cabarets around Pigalle where the lesbianism went no deeper than the butch outfits that the hookers affected.

I auditioned for Suzy Solidor. She said she would have a spot for me come March. And this was November. The next day, my agent called: The owner of the Rupe Tarpea, Rome's biggest club, had caught my audition and wanted to sign me right away.

I was not sorry to get away from Paris. Life with Moustique was becoming unbearable. She got sicker night by night, and her kid would wake up terrified at Moustique's scenes of jealousy, in which she screamed that I didn't love her the way I used to.

Love her—well, those, of course, are the words one has to use. French is so poor in its expressions for love. I had indeed loved the orgasm she had introduced me to, I still loved her lips, her hands, but I had never loved her. Geneviève was the only one who counted. Which, of course, Moustique did not know. She knew Geneviève, but thought we were only good friends. A little butch like her, living with the old traditional stereotypes, could not suspect a love affair between two girls as femme as Geneviève and I both were. As if, in this matter, as in others, clothes made the man.

So I was relieved to get away from Paris. Geneviève had promised to follow me if I could get her a spot, because she did a little singing too.

En route to Rome, in the border tunnel at Modane, I had to fight off an Italian customs man who tried to rape me (I was alone in the compartment, his buddy had obligingly turned off the light, and I can still smell his stench of sweat and leather), but I finally made it okay to Stazione Termini the next morning.

Rome won me over completely. The rooming house they put me up at was nice and comfortable. There I immediately made the conquest of a mysterious individual who insisted on showing me Rome in the highest style, making me get up at the crack of noon so as to see and get to do everything; he took me to the races at Ostia and to the finest restaurants. He gave me a gorgeous ring, and then one morning just left the pensione. He knew I was a lesbian and never made a pass at me, but kept assuring me that when he made his fortune, he would send for me. I'm still waiting.

At the Rupe Tarpea, I was not exactly top banana. I was one of the three band singers, alternating with a very nice Parisian girl strictly the street-urchin or *titi* type, and a beautiful, dark Turkish girl.

I was supposed to be the "ethnic" item, more Cuban than ever; the Parisian *titi* represented the French chanson; and the Turk did the modern stuff. In point of fact, we all did a little bit of everything. We had noticed that the Italians paid no attention whatsoever to what we were singing, so we improvised words or sang well-known bawdy parodies, like the one to the tango "A media luz," that went:

> I may not be too bright,
> But tell me, pretty lass,
> How come so many blond girls
> Have dark hair on their ass . . .

We taught our Turkish friend all kinds of words like these,

and the unsuspecting audiences ate them up. She acquired a very strange brand of French lyrics to take back to Turkey with her.

There was also a young French mistress of ceremonies, perfectly ravishing but unspeakably stupid. For instance, one day she asked me—since I was supposed to be the "intellectual" in the group—how come the Rupe Tarpea had a statue outside of a cow suckling two young babies. I had to explain to her about the legend of Romulus and Remus.

Seeing Rome from a carriage, from the Coliseum to the Forum by way of the Tarpeian Rock, was one long lark, because of the jokes of the Parisian street urchin and the cracks of my ravishing idiot. The Turk didn't always go with us. She was engaged, and faithful to her guy, but being bothered by pressing sexual urges she would spend her days "touching herself," as we taught her to call it, and come to work at night with circles under her eyes halfway down to her chin.

The Rupe Tarpea played to the Roman upper crust. Movie stars on drugs, degenerate princes, drunken upper-class ladies, all of them group-sex freaks, cynical, blasé, acting out *La Dolce Vita* before the fact.

A famous movie comedian held my hand all of one evening, told me all of his troubles, and finally swapped me his gold watch for a piece of the hem of my dress.

And once a Roman countess told me she'd give me a hundred dollars, quite a sum at the time, if I came to tea at her villa on the other side of the Tiber, and made love to her for the delectation of the rich American who was keeping her. I went for the tea, took the hundred, but then tried to get her to take it back, because I just couldn't. But *noblesse oblige*—and she had me driven back home without wincing. She was very beautiful, but awfully old at the time (she must have been all of forty).

There was a French magician on the bill who made passes at me. As a recent and still untutored lesbian, I thought that if I told him what my scene was he'd leave me alone. I still was not aware that most men are wildly turned on by the idea of making it with a lesbian. They think that's an open door to their deepest desire, their most ardent wish, their most common fantasy: to see two women making love and then, of course, to slip in between.

This magician was no exception to the rule.

"But, little one," he conned me, "if you only knew. I make love just like a lesbian!"

I was nonplussed.

"Oh, yes, just listen to this. One time I was on the road with a lesbian. Several weeks had gone by and neither one of us had found anyone to make love with, so one Sunday afternoon, for fun, she made me up, put her skirt, blouse, and shoes on me, and ended up thinking I was really a woman. We made love wonderfully. She got on top of me, she dominated me, and I made like a real pussycat . . ."

I looked wide-eyed at the balding magician with his bulging belly, his aging looks, and tried to imagine him without his glasses, his nearsighted eyes circled with dark shadow, his mouth smeared with lipstick, and the cheapjill lesbian turning on over his hairy body in some hotel room in Limoges or Château-Thierry. And then I told him that that just wouldn't work with me. I could go only for women—real ones.

He sneered, as any man would, "It's only been a year since you last slept with a man. Wait around two or three, and see whether you're still talking the same way . . ."

Well, let's talk about it now, twenty-five years later. I'm celebrating my silver anniversary. Today, when I say I'll never make love with a man again and have gotten along without them for a quarter of a century, they almost believe me. But still not completely. They still hope. They think it is so impossible to do without them totally, entirely. By now, I really ought to be in the clear. There is a statute of limitations, after all. But back then, I was enraged to find so much skepticism, such self-assurance among men. "Nevermore," quoth this raven. But they just laughed.

One morning, outside the room I was sharing with the street urchin, I hear an awful racket. The door bursts open: It's Moustique, tousled and haggard. She throws herself upon me, grabs me by the throat, and screams:

"You were unfaithful, you slut, now choose. Would you rather I slashed your face or cut your hair off?"

I blanch. My street-urchin roommate comes between us. Moustique calms down a bit. She explains.

I had left one of Geneviève's letters lying around and Moustique had found out about us.

What I had not known but now found out was that she too had been sleeping with Geneviève. At first I didn't believe her. But she convinced me by telling me how Geneviève made love. Obviously it must be easier to prove this kind of thing where men are concerned: It must be enough just to describe their equipment, probably no two sets are alike. But for us—it's also fairly easy. Because every woman makes love according to a pattern to which she remains constant. She cries out, or sighs, groans, or murmurs. She squeaks like a mouse or roars like a tigress. She utters the same words at exactly the same moments.

Moustique was not lying. Geneviève had really slept with her. Geneviève had deceived me. She was still sleeping with C. while telling me in letters that he was just a platonic friend. That was why, even though I had finally located a job for her in Rome, she found a thousand ways to put off joining me there. She had lied to me, taken me for a ride. But I would have plenty of time to cry over that. Right now, Moustique was back on the warpath. Before coming down to "disfigure" me, she was mumbling, she had beat Geneviève up, ransacked her apartment, shredded her clothes, busted her telephone, torn up all her papers.

Now it was my turn. My heart was in my boots. Best to show how terrified I was, to assure her of my repentance—and that way I got her into my arms, and knew I was off the hook. Once close to me the little toughie softened up completely and wept over the love she had found again.

My Parisian pal discreetly turned her head to the wall and pretended to be asleep. We made love silently but madly. That same evening, I sent a happy, pacified Moustique back on the Paris train.

But I was desperate. My first *chagrin d'amour*, my first betrayal . . .

I wept copiously—for a few days. But I was in my twenties, had a terrific urge for physical lovemaking, and threw myself into it body and soul in order to forget.

Since then, my whole life, I've retained that same reflex. To keep my heart from bleeding, my head from thinking, the best remedy had always been another girl, another girl right away, because one's mind is occupied while making love. Because the new woman one discovers, even if she is not sensational, is a diversion. Licking one's wounds with endless sniveling never helped anything. One has to bite into life again, as soon as possible, even if it means holding back the tears on an almost unknown shoulder. Diversion-women, consolation-women, port-of-call-between-two-loves-women, I owe much of my happiness in living to you . . .

I decided I'd sleep with the attractive little moron in order to forget Geneviève. Of course, she knew I was a lesbian, as I had not hidden the fact. So I just said, "I'll drop by your hotel to wake you tomorrow afternoon. But you know, I love women, so you'd better watch out."

She accepted my attentions with the greatest of pleasure, at great length, and once my passion had been happily spent, she whispered, looking at me through her long half-closed eyelashes: "Why, it's really true. You weren't lying. You really *are* a lesbian."

Like our Turkish jazz singer, she too was engaged and had promised to be faithful to her man. But her conscience was one that could be easily assuaged. She had promised her fiancé that she would not betray him, which meant she would not have sex with another man. And I was not another man

—*so*, silly and uneducated though she might have been, she was sharp and shrewd enough to rationalize that; she was deliciously all woman!

My contract in Rome was coming to an end. After my disappointment, there was no reason for me to return to Paris and put up with the fight I would have to wage if I were to make a breakthrough in the singing world there. Once again, I ducked out and went to Marseille.

That way, I lost Geneviève, whom I never wanted to see again, and bade goodbye to Moustique, who now felt that she might just as well return to Casablanca.

I got to Marseille on Christmas Eve. Guy was happy. Decently happy, for our relations were not undergoing any change, and he knew it. But I was there, with him, which was what counted.

His father bought us a very small apartment facing the Catalonian Beach: former servants' quarters that had been connected in some grotesque way, but that offered a fine view of the sea.

Guy painted the walls, doors, closets. We lived in a decor of lush jungle alive with unknown flora and strange fauna that leapt up the walls to the ceiling. It was very pretty and very lively.

We had no friends. Our few attempts to socialize with the "young couples" of the Marseille bourgeoisie had turned out to be disastrous. We had nothing in common with them. We had escaped, had known the smell of the greasepaint, the roar of the crowd, the heckling of creditors, Paris, Spain, Africa, hunger, hope, disappointments, heady sensations. We came back to the gilded cage of the establishment with our tails between our legs, true, flayed, bent, but not broken. These wolves had not turned into dogs. We would go on living outside the pale. Our "special" union, moreover, could not fit in to any standard conformism, and rather than shock our peers, we decided we'd do better to avoid them.

Guy would occasionally cruise girls at the Wamping, a dance spot right across from where we lived. It was very convenient: He had only to cross the street to have them in bed.

And I was beginning to find my way around Marseille's gay world. It wasn't high society, of course; the bars in which gay men and lesbians met could not even qualify as café society. In the provinces, gays of any "social standing" have to keep to their closets; too much danger in being found out. So the only ones who come out are those who have nothing to lose, neither position nor reputation. Only a few unconscious men or women like me ventured into the sordid ghetto bars to which gays were restricted. I said "were restricted," because, thank heavens, that situation has greatly improved in the twenty-five years that have passed. Now we have real cafés and discothèques of our own. But then, the stinking cellar, the sordid out-of-the-way joint, the backroom of a crummy pizzeria—these were about all that could be found as a meeting place for fags and dykes. We had so little open to us that we had to settle for almost anything—even in Paris, and of course more so in the provinces.

Today, there are male gay clubs all over and since I opened the Katmandou, lesbians finally have a discothèque of their own worthy of the name, as well appointed and elegant as any comparable straight establishment.

I was quickly spotted as the only middle-class type in these joints. That peculiarity plus my petite physique quickly gained me a host of would-be friends as well as enemies.

I first went with a movie-house usherette, a bit beyond the first flush of youth, and not all that terrific-looking. She lived with a masseuse who was even older; to her I was a lucky piece of tender quail. We would meet between performances in a hotel on the Canebière, or else she made love to me in a box in the theater that she locked from the inside after tipping off her colleagues. I was anxious to make love, I missed it too terribly much, but she appealed to me so little that each time, once out of her arms, I swore this would be the last time, that's how really revolted I was, now that I wasn't turned on any more.

Fortunately, I then met a middle-class woman, the niece of a famous Paris publisher, a noted horsewoman, accomplished skier, much-in-demand rally driver, but really too stinking a lover to imagine. I was beginning to ask myself some troubling questions: Would I ever finally find a woman who was more or less of my social level and knew how to make love? Were those two things so incompatible? Why Geneviève and this woman on the one hand, and Moustique and the movie usherette on the other?

There was one blond newspaperwoman who seemed very old to me then (she was past thirty!), who confessed to eclectic tastes in both men and women. But I was too love-starved to look too closely at that. I met her in a little bar, below where we lived, kept by a funny and charming eccentric dame, where I spent my evenings, when I wasn't immersing myself in the "ghetto bars."

She came up one afternoon. Quick strip, kisses. I begin to caress her. She seemed to be liking it, reacted, moaned, and then suddenly said, "Stop! I don't want to come right away. Let's talk about something else. Did you see such-and-such a film?"

We talked for a while. I start caressing her again. Before getting to the point of no return, same interruption, and this time, we talked about books, the whole thing interlaced with plans for the future, like, "This summer, we'll go swimming across the way at the Catalonians', and I'll suck you off in the cabana," and even rawer expressions of hers that kept turning me off more and more. Finally, I ended up bringing her to a quick climax. She reciprocated by doing me a quite forgettable oral favor, and then she got dressed and left. We both said, "We'll phone." But we never did.

Two years later, Guy picked her up one time and brought her home. That was quite a different story. She yelled and groaned so loud I needed earplugs in order to sleep. He dragged her over the carpet, slapped her, and they put on one hell of a party. One never can really tell whether a woman is going to be a "good lay." That's purely subjective and depends very much on one's own tastes for the ways of love-making as well as hers.

Sex is not all there is in life. I was making love, of course, for whatever it was worth, but one still had to live. Guy didn't earn a great deal. His father remained firm on that point and refused to treat him like the boss's son. We were being made to pay through the nose for our wastrel years!

So, needing a job, I scoured the want ads, without any preconceived notion. I did have a law degree, even if I hadn't taken the bar exams on account of the *Ballets Nègres*. A private religious boarding school for girls, St. Thomas Aquinas, was looking for a history-geography teacher and I filled the bill because they really wanted a history prof who could also double in Spanish for sophomores. Could I? Why, of course! It just happened I was pretty good in that language, too, as I told them. They took my word for it.

I had barely a month to prepare my lessons. I was to have all the classes from the sixth grade through the senior year of high school. Using all kinds of documents and books of varying points of view, I outlined a history course that I think was pretty good.

I remembered the professor I had had as a junior and senior at the Lycée Albert-Sarraut in Hanoi, and that helped. He was an old opium addict, a mad genius, who told us the history of France as if it had been a Western, bringing back to life all the good guys and the bad guys who were otherwise embalmed in the textbooks. I did likewise. My history classes were among the girls' favorites. I made them laugh, and cry, and they loved me for it.

Spanish was something else again! Having knocked around Spain for six months with our *Ballets*, I did have the music of the language well in my ear and mind, and a vocabulary of fifty words or so . . . So, on the very first day, I told the pupils, "Girls, we're going to have a written quiz, so I can find out how much you know."

Of course, I didn't bother to correct their papers; I couldn't have. The next session, I said, "Young ladies, you've forgotten all you knew during vacation. In order to get you off on the right foot this year, we're going to go back to lesson one and do a quick review."

I crammed, keeping two or three lessons ahead of them. By the end of the year I had caught up to them and gotten ahead. The next year, I was able to teach Spanish to the seniors in high school.

To be truthful, not all the teachers were as "sharp" as I, and the girls, knowing that in these private schools they hired just about anybody to teach any old thing, had their fun at the beginning of the year by asking trick questions, to see whether they could trip us up. The nun who had taught history before me had lost face completely by assuring them that Cape Horn was what the English called the Cape of Good Hope.

Another year, they asked me to teach junior physics. In this case I struck out trying to keep one lesson ahead of the class. I have so little aptitude for anything in the remotest way connected with math and am so turned off by figures of any kind, those ugly twisted little earthworms, that after two months I was completely at sea, and had to ask to be relieved of that course.

Her name was Carole.

One day, as I was arriving at school at the wheel of my little car, I saw a ravishing short-haired brunette with a perfect face and the carriage of a queen walking up the street. I turned to admire her. "It wouldn't be my luck to have that kind of a girl in one of my classes," I sighed to myself. I parked. To my surprise, she went into the school. I followed, and saw her merge into the group of seniors. Only then did I see her: for two months, she had been in front of me every day, but she wore glasses and I simply hadn't *seen her*.

The first chance I got, I approached her.

"If you want to do me a favor," I said, "from now on in my classes, at least during oral quizzes, would you please not wear your glasses?"

She agreed, though a little surprised. Later, I asked her to have tea with me on the way home.

That was the start of a sweet relationship. I never hid what I was from her, though I assured her immediately that my intentions were purely honorable.

For a year, we went out on Sundays, toward Cassis or La Ciotat, with Guy. Carole used to come over to our apartment to visit and we would have dinner together. When there was no school, she would spend entire afternoons lying alongside me. She snuggled into my arms and we talked. I told her my life story, helped her review her subjects. Sometimes, there was a moment of silence, both of us turned on. But never, never did I make any direct pass at her. She would have let me. She loved me, as I loved her. But we never let it show.

With her, there was the perfect symbiosis of my adolescent loves and my grownup passions. I could still love without desiring, because she was my pupil, because she was only sixteen and I twenty-four. I had no right to steer her life into a course which is not that of the majority.

Yet Carole was not a virgin. She had been with two boys. But that did not reduce my scruples any. I have never met a single lesbian teacher who slept with one of her pupils.

We are no more danger to the morals of an adolescent girl than a married man with a family who might fall for one of his students. Perhaps even much less, because we know that our gate is strait and we do not try to push anyone through it.

The next year, on Christmas Eve, I found Carole waiting when school let out. She was terribly upset. "My mother found out about you from friends in Casablanca," she said. "She has forbidden me ever to see you again."

We were floored. I took her to tea for one last time, at a pastry shop near the school. With tears in her eyes, she assured me that come what might she would go on seeing me, that she couldn't stand not to.

She came over two days later. I hugged her. We silently savored our happiness. There was a violent knock at the door. It was her mother, who had followed her. "Madame," I told her, "I don't understand this ban. I am what I am, but I have never laid a finger on Carole."

"I know. I've read all your letters."

"Then why keep her from seeing me?"

"Because you are a bad influence. For her reputation, it is just not permissible. If you see her again, I will have to denounce you to the mother superior."

That was it, I was a plague carrier. Merely seeing me could spread the disease. I was infected with galloping Sapphism.

I lost Carole. But four years later she got married, and the first thing she did as a married woman was to invite me to lunch—along with her mother. The latter was civil to me. Now I could have slept with her daughter, and had her blessing to boot, for Carole had been married off, was respectable and her reputation saved.

But after four years, alas, even the fondest of loves can fade, and Carole remained for me what she had become: a tender memory.

One evening I was having an apéritif at the Cancan, a so-called American bar run by Alice Guerini, where I met the group of waitresses, salesgirls, and so on, that I generally went with, to the great displeasure of Guy, who thought I was degrading myself. I noticed a somewhat plump pretty little brunette, a bit affected, who stood out from the lot.

We were both standing at the bar, separated by a large

bouquet of gladioli. I start a conversation, discover she is twenty-two, a nurse, named Maïna. Large dark eyes, a seductive smile, a few winks, and I'm hooked. Then she moves away, a little high, although it is only eight in the evening.

I go over to a detestable butch, one who wears padded shoulders so as to swagger around like a pimp, with a cigarette butt dangling from her lips, and two broads turned out on the bricks hustling to support her.

"Who is that gal, José?"

"Interests you, ha? That was obvious! Oh, she's all right, all right. They say she screws pretty good."

"Did you—uh, sleep with her?"

"No, not me. But I know a married couple who swung with her."

The following Saturday I see her again, at a party at the home of that society woman rally driver. Drunk again, petting left and right. She is really very, very pretty. Lying on a sofa in a dark corner, she is doing some real heavy necking with Claire, the hairdresser. When the latter comes back toward us, hair mussed and blouse askew, she is shaking herself off like a hen after the rooster has had at her. "What a house on fire, that little dame!"

I did not go near her that evening. I was supposed to be our hostess's date and I don't like to play dirty tricks on those I am close to. But when she was leaving, I helped her on with her coat, and whispered in her ear, "I'll be waiting for you at my place tomorrow afternoon at four. It's 8 Rue des Catalans, top floor."

She came. I was ready for her, nude under a djellabah, to save time. I hate the act of undressing, it turns me off. And besides, she seemed so easy that I thought there was no need for fancy lead-ins.

As soon as she came in, I drew her to me, shoved her over on the bed, and gave her a long kiss. A house on fire, indeed!

She took my face in her hands, and said, "I love you."

I smiled superciliously, like a detestable little Doña Juana, and answered, "No, just say you want me. That's not love. Not that!"

I kissed her again. Then we made love, with multiple delights. It was March 30. The day before my twenty-fifth birthday. She was a most exciting present.

Very quickly I fell in love with Maïna. But that swinging group-sex story bothered me. I would not be able to love her fully unless I knew she was really sincere with me. I was quite willing to forgive, but first I wanted her to confess her "sins." Soiled she might be, but limpid in my eyes.

One day, after lovemaking, while she was resting huddled in my arms, I went at it.

"I love you," I told her, "and I don't want to hide any of my past from you. It's not very pretty, and I'm not proud of it, but you have to know about it."

She looked at me, pained, worried.

"Do you really think I have to?"

"Absolutely. The fact is, I made love with a couple, a man and a woman."

"Oh, no, be quiet, keep still," she moaned.

I kept hammering away. I wanted to hear her say, "Oh, it's not important. Don't torture yourself over that. I've done the same thing."

To give her a chance to shed her guilt before me, I was denigrating myself. I could give her no greater proof of my love. But she confessed nothing. So I finally told her the truth. At first, she was dumbfounded, but then she really flew off the handle.

"That's a horrible thing!" she countered. "It's ridiculous! To think you would hurt me like that for nothing! How could you ever have believed that José? She made up that story because she never could get anywhere with me. That very evening, at the Cancan, when I first saw you, I asked her who you were. You interested me. She didn't like that a bit. So she told me that you were being screwed by your husband. I was afraid, the first time that I came up here, but you attracted me so much . . . And *I* didn't really believe her!"

Maïna was selfish, a tease, fiery, a spoiled kid, tender, loving. We adored each other for over three years. She really was my first great love, a love finally shared, fully, without clouds. We lived together, we shared everything, just like any other couple.

Guy lived with us. He went his own way, had his passing love affairs, and was glad to see me happy at last, settled with Maïna, whom he liked very much. When the three of us went out together, people noticed us, and it made him proud in a way.

When I first met Maïna, she had been about to marry a young Corsican doctor. Breaking off with him was a trauma. He could not understand, would not accept it. He broke into her room and waited for her there during a whole weekend. But she didn't show up. She practically didn't live there any more. Out of rage and impatience, he smashed her few belongings. Pictures were torn up, clothes scissored to bits, drug capsules carefully emptied down the drain—the works. Seeing what he had done, I was reminded of Moustique's revenge against Geneviève. Spite and low blows aren't limited to any one sex.

He phoned Guy to tell him his wife was a lesbian slut who had corrupted his fiancée. He got told off, of course. Guy laughed about it all, finding it priceless. He was probably gratified at seeing another man put down by the Amazons. Fate was giving him a revenge of a sort and he felt no male solidarity with the furious little Corsican.

For over a month, we went out only by way of the cellar, because her fiancé stood guard outside our front door, for hours on end, day and night, watching from his little gray car.

Finally he disappeared.

Maïna's mother had lived with another woman for ten years. She was the one who had initiated her. Maïna had slept with only one man, this doctor, and had decided to marry him for security, not because she loved him, and especially not that he climaxed her. She had met him on the rebound after her girl friend, another nurse like her, had dropped her to go to Gabon and get married. She was fed up with girls. She had been so hurt, had felt so betrayed, so abandoned.

And then she met me. When she said "I love you" to me that first day, she had really meant it. But I hadn't believed her, and that hurt her so that it was months before she said it to me again.

We were happy together. Maïna had stopped drinking, she didn't need that escape any more. We had a nice apartment, a small car, and our two salaries allowed us to live if not in luxury at least well enough.

Little by little, we had finally found a circle of more interesting women friends: professors, teachers, painters, antique dealers. Most of them lived in or around Aix-en-Provence.

At the studio of the painter Vincent Roux, we met Hélène, a superbourgeoise of the old nobility of Aix. She was twenty, full of charm, her eyes sparkling with mischief. She was fascinated by the unconcern and naturalness with which Maïna and I allowed ourselves to be seen together in public. Without trying to shock, we would hold hands if we felt like it, and our eyes said enough so that no one needed to question what went on between us. At the end of the evening, she asked if she could see me, "to talk about important things."

In a café on the Old Port, she confessed to me, "I feel that I am a lesbian like you. But I don't dare make a start. I don't know how to go about it. I'm afraid that if I'm attracted to a woman she will turn me down."

I thought I was hearing myself talk back in Casablanca, when I first was in love with Geneviève, and got my first lessons from Moustique.

I answered her. And twenty years later, every time we see each other, she still reminds me of it with gratitude.

"You told me, 'Plunge right in! At any rate, with women, if you plunge, you'll always make out. They don't resist very long.'

"And so I plunged—and you were right, it always worked."

And even today Hélène is still the greatest ladies'-woman of Aix and the surrounding areas.

The irony of it is that I myself am unable to follow the advice I so convincingly gave her. When a woman really attracts me, I become bashful, awkward, I lose my voice, and if I do jump in, I'm like a kid off the high diving board, covering my eyes and ears. That is not a calculated tactic. It's just plain timidity. Most of the time, I don't dare make the first move, unless she has given me some encouragement, by a look, or a sign.

Our life went by without any dramatic upsets, just some violent, futile fights because we both had stormy dispositions, but these blew over in a hurry.

We sometimes went to Nice to see her family. Her mother was now married to a nice enough tolerant policeman, who accepted us very easily. Her sister, France, as blond as Maïna was dark, had steel-blue eyes, and stared adamantly, hostilely at me. Seeing the two sisters together, France was the one who might have been taken for a lesbian. Her tomboy manner, brusque gestures, short hair, even the way she lit her cigarette lacked all femininity.

She too had grown up with her mother and the latter's lesbian friend. But where Maïna had accepted that way of life as her own, her sister had acquired its external mannerisms but rejected the life itself.

Yet I am sure that the more inverted of the two was France: She had no boy friends, only poor pale imitations, just her Vespa, her fishing, her volleyball—poor France!

In the summer, we would spend our vacations with Guy and whatever mistress he had at the time. We drove about in Spain, in Italy, in a large open Delahaye touring car, young, thoughtless, carefree. But then Guy would begin to act up. In Marseille, he rarely kept a girl for more than a week. He took them, enjoyed them, and rejected them. On vacation, their presence quickly bored him. We would try to be nice to the poor girl, to make up for his growing incivility to her, when he was always so sweet and thoughtful to Maïna and me. But by the end of the second week, the girl would have thought up some excuse for taking off. Guy was delighted to put her on a train, and the three of us then finished our holidays together, happy as three kids.

At the end of three years at St. Thomas Aquinas, I was fired. No reason given. The superior just called me in and, after many circumlocutions, told me she could not keep me on: "You do not correspond to what our house expects its teachers to be."

I did not need any additional explanation. I had understood very well. For a year now, I had known through Carole that there were rumors about me. The students, who were fond of me, had unwittingly hurt me. They all talked about me too often at home. Much too often, so that the parents finally were intrigued and wanted to know more about this exotic bird their daughters were so taken with. And, since Marseille is after all only a provincial city, one day it all came together: "Madame—why—she's that industrialist's wife who— What a horror! She's going to pervert our innocent children!"

And the Parents' Association took it up forthwith with the mother superior.

I left St. Thomas Aquinas heartsick and, for a change of pace, put in a couple of years teaching primary grades, still in a religious school, of course, since I didn't have public-school certification.

I taught fifth and sixth grades. Quite a difference from the almost grown-up young ladies at St. Thomas. I had forty kids, aged seven to ten. A working-class neighborhood, the parents simple, naive, open-minded. The little girls were adorable, virgin soil to educate, cultivate, awaken. Fascinating. Very quickly, the little girls started showering me with gifts: sticky candies wrapped in a piece of toilet tissue, anonymous flowers dropped on my desk, eggs brought in from the country. We spent six hours a day together. It was trying work, even less well paid than the other, but so engrossing.

A class one likes, when taken in hand, becomes a homogeneous whole, an entity with its own character, virtues, and faults, just like a human being. Relationships of strength, love, or hatred are set up on an equal-to-equal basis. With my children it was a marriage of love. And they could talk about me at home as much as they liked: in those circles, there was no chance of anyone recognizing the wayward wife of the Marseille bourgeoisie and pointing a finger at her.

Guy and I were now living in that "Radiant City" named after Le Corbusier, in a wonderful building complex designed for comfort and good living. On the twenty-second floor. As one comes in, the sea, the islands, the beach are all there to fill the eyes.

Guy took up with a neighbor on the same floor. Jocelyne was a superb, exuberant blonde, slightly flighty, who had an adorable little black girl whom she left with a wet nurse. Jocelyne told us that on her eighteenth birthday, in Africa where her father was a colonel, a black guest of his had prevailed upon her to sit on his lap, and taken advantage of the situation to force his attentions on her.

She was being kept by the managing director of a big company and occasionally moonlighted with a few "tricks" for pocket money. She asked me to help her get taken on as a teacher at my school. I had some misgivings on the subject, but she kept at it so hard that I finally recommended her for the next term. Maybe she really did want to change her way of life. Anyway, the mother superior liked her and hired her on the spot.

There might be much to be said pro and con about this kind of a school with a whore and a lesbian on its faculty. But we did our jobs well and could explain the rule of three to our charges just as well as any straight teacher whose life-style was above social censure.

Obviously, I couldn't help smiling at the strange setup. I often thought of it, during chapel, which we had every day. Especially when Jocelyne didn't take her lunch in the canteen and rushed back afterward winking at me. She had found a dependable "trick" at the end of the block; twice a week she would go over and give the bike dealer a blow job.

But she didn't last long as a teacher. It's tough to work six hours a day. It interfered with her call-girl avocation, and she quit. Guy and I were her only friends, so she kept us filled in on the ups and downs of her life in great detail.

One day she got a letter from an electric-range salesman named Roger, who said he had been recommended by a friend. From time to time his work brought him to Marseille and he would like to meet her. The letter was most courteous and she naturally answered it. But with each letter his tone changed, the style got racier, the allusions more precise, until they became outspokenly obscene.

Jocelyne was no *enfant de Marie*, but soon it was more than even she could stomach. So as soon as she got a letter from Roger, she would rush over and read it to us. We died laughing over them. Guy and I would dictate answers to her, just as sizzling as his questions had been. With pen poised in the air, she would mutter, "No, I can't write that, really!"

"Write," we commanded.

We had her slip into the letters hunks of gauze or cotton that she told him she had worn all day inside her panties, and other refinements of this sort. Roger was very poetical. He found the right words to explain how, by doing a handstand against his bedroom wall while he masturbated, he was able to savor his own semen.

Jocelyne shivered.

"Good God! It'll be some kind of a session when that character shows up. Talk about kinky!"

Finally Roger did set a date for coming in. At the prearranged time, I was behind our door, which was slightly ajar so as to see him go by. I would have given a lot to follow him on in. But what I saw come up was a fat, harmless fifty-year-old with gold-rimmed glasses.

A bare half hour later, Jocelyne burst into our place, out of breath, relieved, and hilarious. The silly hick had put her on her back, given a quick swipe at her tits, and shot his load in no time after a few dull push-and-pulls. Then he had left, fully satisfied, as quietly as he had come.

Good old Roger could only make it big in the porno-letter department.

That was how three happy years went by. I thought it would last forever, all my life. I wasn't looking for any other woman. We were faithful to each other. We had no bone to pick with each other, we were a model couple. Young, both very femme, with long hair, Maïna's in a low bun, mine braided on the side, both of us dark-skinned, we were often taken for sisters.

Five years after she had left, Annie, Maïna's ex-girl friend, came back from Gabon. The marriage had flopped, normal life had not worked out, she wanted back into Maïna's life, and expected to shack up with her again, sweeping aside my three-year interlude. There didn't seem to me to be much danger of that. I was sure of our love and trusted Maïna.

But the other one started a slow, persistent undermining job. She came after Maïna at the clinic, where they had previously worked together and she was on familiar ground.

"How can you put up with that ménage à trois? If Elula really loves you, why won't she leave her husband? Because she's more interested in her own security and comfort. You come second. She doesn't think about your future; and you don't have any husband to take care of you."

A fine thing! She was a good one to be talking about the security of marriage!

At the start, I just smiled and shrugged my shoulders. I never would have dreamed of forbidding Maïna to meet her, or of going after her for a confrontation. I abhor those demeaning melodramatic scenes.

But just then was when Geneviève reappeared. I don't know how she had traced me. I gave her a surprised and glacial reception.

"I wanted to ask you what had happened," she said.

"After five years?"

"I don't understand why you did what you did, why you never came back to Paris from Rome."

"It doesn't matter any longer. That's all long past and over. I'm happy, I'm living with a girl I love. I don't want to hear any more about what may have gone on way back then."

I slammed the door. Geneviève left in tears. She had become an actress and I sometimes saw her name on a theater poster or in TV drama credits.

Maïna worked days at the clinic and took on more and more night duty so as to be able to buy her own car. She was exhausted, unstrung. She was losing weight and looked like a little skinned cat; and her disposition reflected it: She had become very edgy. Annie's undermining campaign began to bear fruit. Our love was showing chinks. They now sometimes went out together. I finally lost my temper and had to say to her: As long as you're going with your old friend, there's no reason why I shouldn't see Geneviève.

We planned to go to Paris for the Easter vacation. I wrote Geneviève at the TV station and suggested we see each other. She accepted enthusiastically.

Maïna had not blinked at the idea of this reunion. But when Geneviève came to pick me up, it was another story. When she saw her through the window coming for me, as blond and beautiful as ever, the jealous female broke out in Maïna. She rushed at me just after I had said a tender good-night to her. She grabbed me by the hair and we rolled on the ground; I had to hold her hands to try and keep her from scratching me. We struggled silently, because my family was in the next room. I finally got away. On the stairs, trembling with rage, I redid my braid. I could feel a big scratch burning my neck.

I had had no intention at all of sleeping with Geneviève. I had just wanted to make Maïna jealous. I thought that this reunion with Geneviève might keep Maïna and me together. But her behavior had revolted me. So, to get even, I did make love with Geneviève. She was as witty and entertaining as ever. She knew fascinating people whom she introduced me to: Marcel Camus, Boris Vian. I went backstage at theaters with her, attended TV rehearsals, she opened an undreamed-of world to the little backwater schoolteacher I had become.

Maïna had gone back to Marseille before me, the day after our rassling match, penitent, and full of good intentions. After the holidays, I went back too. But something had snapped. There were constant scenes between us now. Annie had succeeded: The relationship was breaking down. One day, finally the catastrophe happened. Maïna threw a tantrum, smashing the TV screen, jumping on me again, suddenly ten times her normal strength out of rage, and if a gay man we were going to have dinner with hadn't arrived just then, I don't know what might have happened. He succeeded in getting her into his car and back to the clinic where she worked. She was given a sedative and put to bed.

We were supposed to leave the next day for Saint-Tropez, just the two of us, for Guy had had a little lung trouble and been at Courchevel for the past three months. We had rented a little shack among the grapevines, on the road to Tahiti. We had been dreaming of this vacation for half a year. Our bags were packed.

The night was a long one. I couldn't make sense of all that had happened. Maïna had insulted me, deserted me, and said she was going back to Annie. I wired Guy asking for help. I was unhappy, I was alone.

I couldn't sleep. The silence at the Le Corbusier became intolerable. I needed to talk to a human being. Night people are more accessible and less conformist than day people, whatever their professions. I phoned the morning wake-up service, highway information, long-distance directory, the telegraph office. I got two nice guys and I talked to them for several hours. About everything, about nothing. They would put me on hold and come back to me after answering other calls.

Like Monsieur Seguin's goat in the Alphonse Daudet story, I fought it out all night, and at dawn Maïna no longer existed for me. I wanted nothing more to do with her; a spring inside me had snapped. I had no more love, no more sorrow, no hatred, merely emptiness, a great void. I was a felled oak with no more feelings than a tree struck by lightning.

The next morning, a friend named Antoine drove me to Saint-Tropez. Maïna had carried off the registration and keys to my car, saying that three years of enslavement beside me had earned her at least that.

Antoine had been a friend for a long time. He had often taken us to dinner and knew just where I stood. But men still remain wolves, even when they try to hide their fangs. The fangs are always there, just waiting to be revealed.

He was driving me down to help me out, but at the Club Hôtel de Cavalaire he tried to convince me to spend the weekend with him, "in order to console yourself, to forget, to prove to yourself that there are some nice, thoughtful, understanding men in the world."

I heard him out as I picked at my grilled sea perch. My head felt heavy, my eyes smarted behind the dark glasses. On the beach, at our feet, water and sun played gaily. It was vacation time. Rotten vacation, wasted vacation . . .

"Stop the bullshit, Antoine. Yop know you're wasting your time. Just take me on to Saint-Tropez."

Guy had come running as soon as he got my wire. It was not a prudent thing to do, as he was still weak, but he had lost no time in driving down to me, crazy with worry. He stayed with me for two days, just long enough to make sure I was not doing anything silly. He wanted to make me feel he was still with me, and always would be.

Geneviève came to the rescue too, with an actor friend, Sacha Briquet, whose jokes and pranks soon had me laughing.

There was also my old pal Nicky, a pretty schoolteacher who made musical puns, and had a little boat in which we went fishing in the gulf.

Félix, of L'Escale, was there too, cruising Nicole, a gorgeous tease with green eyes, just as I was, but she later left us both high and dry to go and marry a Portuguese millionaire. For now, the three of us would have lunch together at Tahiti, an inexpensive restaurant where you were comfortable because it was so uncrowded.

But I was desperate to forget Maïna. My same old self-defense mechanism: one woman to make me forget another.

A German boy I had met told me, "I know a very beautiful girl who likes women and is alone. Do you want to meet her?"

"What do you think?"

Marie-Laure d'H. was nothing to fall into a faint over, but as a lifebuoy she would do. A fine body, ordinary face with little mousy eyes, a wonderfully gravelly voice, and an insolent manner.

A quarter of an hour later I was at her place for a drink, and half an hour after that we were getting our clothes back on. The apartment had a wide opening on the little port of La Ponche. Her naked body, head thrown back, lighted merely by the distant glimmers of Sainte-Maxime and the moonlight, might have been wonderful. But Marie-Laure made love like a wham-bam-thank-you-ma'am rabbit, squeaking like an ecstatic bunny when she came.

We were not together long, for she had to return to Paris that same evening. I promised to phone her. She had a small dress shop in the Faubourg Saint-Honoré and was being kept by the very rich manufacturer of a famous brand of perfume.

I returned to Marseille at the end of August. I had had no word of Maïna and looked for none.

I learned that she had been very ill. She had been given the sleep treatment. Once recovered, she lived with Annie for a week, and then left her. She could not understand why I refused to get back together with her. She still loved me. She didn't know that to me a love once wounded is doomed to die.

I felt sorry for her, so disoriented and all alone in her little room at the clinic. It hurt in the warm feeling I still held for her, but I was detached. I didn't love her any more.

There was a guy we used to meet at the café, Robert, who for three years had been dying of love for her. He had a cute mug like a cocker spaniel's with sad eyes that made him look like a whipped dog. He would have liked Maïna's delicate little hands to beat him up. He carried on about that while we stuffed ourselves on his caviar and champagne. For his birthday, more hangdog than ever, he asked my permission for Maïna to give him the gloves she was wearing. They were a pair of old kids. In exchange, he slipped me enough money to keep her in mittens till the end of her days. We liked him because he was nice and his simple fantasies entertained us without getting to us.

After we split up, he tried his luck. For several months, he showered her with gifts and supplied her with enough cash so she didn't have to work until she was fully recovered.

She allowed him a few intimacies. He licked her feet and her legs, and asked her to insult him, and then he ejaculated sadly inside his shorts.

Maïna gave me all the details. We saw each other very infrequently, but she made long phone calls to me, and spent her nights putting love notes on the windshield of the

Dauphine that Guy had bought me. I had not tried to get my old car back from her. I hate arguing over possessions, or any kind of money problems. Between two beings who love or have loved one another, money is an obscene intruder.

When I heard about her carryings-on with Robert, I threw a furious fit. Maïna was still too close to my heart for me to tolerate her being defiled. Maïna nude with a man—ugh!

I went all over town telling about Robert and his pitiful way of making do with my leftovers.

Maïna didn't try to stop me; she was delighted and hoped she might win me back through the gambit of jealousy. In fact, she succeeded so well that I finally made a date with her for one night at Cannes. In a cheap hotel room, we made love together again.

She had become a stranger. I no longer knew the clothes she wore, her panties, her bra. They were things bought without me, after me, outside our old universe. Even her body, it seemed, I did not know, or else I knew it too well. It had the dull taste of a dish heated over, barely lukewarm.

I pretended to come, and so did she. We were polite. We didn't wish to hurt one another. Our movements were mechanical; they had no more soul. We had made love together much too well to be satisfied with a mere reminder.

A short time after that, on the terrace of a café, she met a young fellow who told her he was a plantation manager in Guinea. He was leaving forty-eight hours later. She accepted his impetuous proposal. The next night he took her to his hotel, to screw at least once before he left, just to see whether it would work.

After four years Maïna returned to intercourse without too much displeasure, and she sailed for Guinea as soon as he sent her the ticket.

But the guy turned out not to be the plantation manager —at best, only an assistant overseer. After a month of marriage, Maïna left him, settled in Conakry, and went to work for a physician, who became her second husband. They had a little girl. I found all this out from the letters she wrote me, even though I never answered them. When she told me she had become a mother, I felt that I should at least drop her a line. To tell her to stop writing. I was not interested. The life of a housewife in Guinea was of as much interest to me as that of a Martian.

She stopped.

She must be well into her forties, still an enticing tease, a child-woman past her prime, and many a man—not to mention woman—must have loved that adorable spoiled child, even as I myself had.

CHAPTER

IV

As my book of hours with Maïna came to its close, I also decided to go back to secondary-school teaching. Primary was just too hard. I resumed history-geography courses at two other religious institutions, and soon was immersed in a new "idyll" with Catherine, a tenth-grade student.

She was blond, beautiful, willowy, and as stupid as my Carole at St. Thomas had been bright. She was barely sixteen, and no longer a virgin. Neither backward nor shy, she was soon making clear, if naive, advances to me.

"I know a girl my age who is very much like me and would like to meet a woman like you, of your age. Would you know anyone who . . . ?"

I pretended not to understand. As with Carole, nothing happened between us. I never even hugged her tenderly. I liked her for her beauty, but she was too stupid to appeal to me. I enjoyed going out with her as one enjoys showing off a fine jewel or pretty fur. I tried to teach her a little something about life, all with the blessing of her father, a colonel who was happier to see her out with me than with boys.

He was right. I kept her from an affair with a married man with children. I taught her not to go to bed with every Tom, Dick, and Harry in exchange for a dinner or a weekend. I tried to put a bit of order and moral sense into her tiny brain. Maybe I succeeded, maybe not. She left Marseille shortly after that. Catherine had lasted only one fall season.

I had found out through her that a girl in her class was madly in love with me. A real little budding lesbian, boyish, with short hair, unrefined, not too pretty, with a hustling eye. She didn't hesitate to say before her classmates, "I'd like to take Elula in my arms and kiss her everywhere, just everywhere." I had laughed about it with Catherine. But ever since, whenever I went into their classroom, I felt a little embarrassed, although it wasn't an unpleasant feeling to be the object of this innocent desire, this ardent and silent tribute, the pure passion of a child.

I also gave French lessons at the École Pigier business college, to girls sixteen to twenty years old who were studying to become stenographers. They were very nice and we got along fine. My only trouble was with the custodian: I looked so young, despite my tight professorial hair bun, that he consistently took me for a student and wanted to make me check in and out.

That year, I also taught a class of boys there, ranging from thirteen to sixteen years of age. Right off, it didn't work. The desk on the dais was not enclosed, but was just an ordinary table. I could feel the more sophisticated pupils immediately fixing their eyes on my legs, savoring them in every detail. Then their necks twisted as they tried to pry up higher. So I had to give all my courses with legs crossed and my jaws clenched. The looks of those apprentice male stenographers felt like so many sticky leeches on me; they disgusted me so that I, who was used to being a nice, well-liked teacher, firm but flexible, turned into a dry, cold bitch. There was no rapport between me and the class, and after two weeks I asked no longer to have to teach the boys.

As for my love life, well, I was just tooling around, catching what I could where I could. Not in Marseille itself, however, because the people one met in the ghetto bars were still not exactly out of Burke's Peerage.

Every vacation, I would take off in my car. Eleven hours later (this was before the time of the expressways), I would be at my mother's in Paris, grab a quick bath, and rush out to the Trois Fontaines.

That Three Fountains was the "in" lesbian joint of the moment. None of them lasted very long, for a simple reason: An explorer looking for a herd of lesbians to observe or to hunt would have been hard put to locate one. For, at the time of day when lions go to the water hole, when in Tokyo, Paris, or New York, male homosexuals gather in a multitude of bars (listed in a number of guidebooks that are regularly updated), there is virtually no such place for lesbians. No bars, no restaurants, no discothèques. For example, right now there are two or three such *boîtes* in Paris, one in Athens, two in Amsterdam, one in London, one in Brussels, two in New York, two in Los Angeles, a larger number in Germany, though the one in Rio is no longer in existence. Whereas there are half a hundred spots for gay men in Paris, and almost a dozen in Athens.

Why such a difference between the two castes?

Women go out less because they don't enjoy displaying themselves in public places where they might be seen by their bosses and lose their jobs, or at best find themselves at their mercy.

So unless the club is ultra exclusive, the only lesbians to be found there are those who have little to lose: salesgirls, party girls, just-above-working-class types. The lesbian of a higher social background would not set foot in them. For, unlike gay men, lesbians have not yet done away with social distinctions. A butcher boy with a "big jock" can really do well for himself; if he's smart, doesn't blow his nose on the back of his hand, and knows how to "rap" properly, he can end up owning two butcher shops, or even turn decorator or antique dealer. He's bound to find some filthy-rich old geezer who will keep him or stake him to what it takes to go up in the world.

On the other hand, a delightful little salesgirl may meet a woman who will help her lead a different kind of life for a few months or a few years. But she'll never make a spectacular social climb. Among lesbians, princesses don't wed shepherd girls. We have trouble enough hanging on to our own places on the social ladder, so we can hardly help our friends to be upwardly mobile.

Nor will she be kept in great style, for men are generally the ones who have the means for that, and the few well-heeled women one meets don't like being made to pay. We have too much respect for love to feel it can be bought. And besides, we're too clearheaded to be taken in the way male pigeons are. I've only really known three or four lesbians who made it by playing the gigolo (or should one say gigolette?) to silver threads among the gold.

Moreover, while meeting places may be a must for the men, they are less so for us. Gay men have intense constant sexual activity and are always on the lookout for new encounters, so they need a lot of hunting grounds that provide new stock. Whence the proliferation of bars, cafés, nightclubs, restaurants, and well-established pickup spots such as the Tuileries, the Esplanade at the Invalides, and the last remaining *vespasiennes* or other public urinals. They strike up a conversation and ten minutes later they're getting each other off in a car or under some hidden doorway.

Two women rarely end up together on their first night. We don't make love out of simple sheer physical need to ejaculate, and we surround the thing with a few ribbons, that may be termed modesty, shyness, outdated romanticism, or superfluous hypocrisy, according to one's cynicism or credulity.

Perhaps lesbians would get out more if we had truly exclusive clubs such as the ones in the U.S. or London, for instance, to which men simply are not admitted.

In France, that can't be. Unlike the Anglo-Americans, who have a much higher standard of living and like to drink for the pleasure of it, Frenchwomen have little taste for strong liquor and even less money to spend. In order to make it, a lesbian club therefore has to admit some of the moneyholders, that is to say, men, who cluster at the doors like flies around a honey cake.

Little by little, they infiltrate, in larger and larger numbers, until one day they become so visible with their dark jackets and solid shoulders hogging the banquettes and their ungainly jerky dancing that the lesbians quietly start to leave the place in order to go to another club, where the same process then sets in. For in no time at all there will be men sniffing at the door to that one, with their doglike flair for picking up our scent.

It takes a lot of determination and constant vigilance to maintain the proper proportion of men friends required while not exceeding the threshold for what's tolerable. It mainly takes a lot of intuition and very solid judgment to let in only men who are sharp enough to understand that they are on alien soil and that they have to check their little cocked gun at the cloakroom. We have finally been able to work out just that for the last eight years, at the *boîte* that I run in Paris, the Katmandou.

But this was still back in 1958 at the Trois Fontaines, a long narrow barroom with a jukebox giving out with "Come prima," "Fever," and Paul Anka records. The Who's Who of Parisian lesbianism was there: models, actresses, society women, and middle- and upper-echelon whores. Too many men already, patting your fanny and telling you there were thirty thousand francs in it for you if you let them watch you make love to their wives.

That was where I spent evenings as a love-hungry provincial on the prowl.

And where I found Ingrid. A beautiful, long Swede, and of course a fashion model. We went for each other right off.

But she was not much of a lover. Another violin with a

thin sound. Lesbos! Lesbos! What crimes are committed in thy name, and how few consummate consuming lovemakers there are!

There was Viviane, whom I had met at Michou's, at that time just a nighttime bar-restaurant. We had had a lot of laughs together the previous summer at Saint-Tropez. The tourists, who came down hoping to see Bardot, paid plenty of attention to Michou with his ultrashort briefs, his peroxided hair, and his ostentatious beauty. They snapped as many pictures of him as they did of Coin-Coin on his bike or the yachts in the marina.

That evening, Ingrid and I were in there for a late supper. A whole gang of transvestites, fugitives from Madame Arthur's, were also in the place. Among them, one very handsome platinum blond, fire in his eyes, classical profile, looking more like a sophisticated boyish girl than the phony vamp that most drag queens seem.

We smiled at each other. As I passed near him, on the way out, I said, "You're very handsome."

"Thanks," he smiled back. "You're very beautiful too."

An exchange of compliments leading to nothing: just a disinterested tribute, glancingly paid, without ulterior motive.

Then Ingrid remembered she had forgotten her gloves and went back inside. She came out again, shaking with laughter:

"You know what your platinum-blond drag queen told me? He said: 'Tell your friend I'm a girl, not a boy.' "

I bounced right back in to apologize, saying, "You're so beautiful, and that's so unusual for a boyish-type girl . . ."

"No offense," she replied. And she smiled at me with her dazzling teeth, her sensuous mouth.

Obviously, the next night I was back—without Ingrid. Obviously she too showed up for the date we hadn't made.

We had a three-day flirtation. She was a dancer, a stripper, or a whore, or probably a little of each. She had a gorgeous body and haughty, defiant marble breasts.

When we finally made love, Viviane caressed me quite

awkwardly, and would not let me do her in turn. To me, that was an unthinkable attitude. Two lesbians making love are two women making love, two people making love in full equality. They don't split up into one "passive" and the other "active." Sure, one may be more aggressive than the other, more ardent, more daring, and that is the one who most often will take the initiative in life as well as in bed (but that need not always be the one with the shorter haircut).

But there are a few resistant ones who reject any caressing. Thank the Lord, that's rare, and it's ridiculous. A man lets a woman stroke or kiss him without losing his sense of dominance. So I can't stomach women who take themselves for guys and reject any caressing to prove their virility!

In others, very often it is just shyness, or a block that one fine night will give way before a sweetheart with enough patience and talent. But not in Viviane's case. She "flexed her muscles" like a real tough from the Pigalle tenderloin. She was so convinced that she was a gentleman of leisure, or reasonable facsimile thereof, that she murmured sweet nothings to me, like "You're really my sweet gal; I go for you hook, line, and sinker. I'd never turn you out on the bricks to hustle; you're my own sweet little woman."

She delighted me with that kind of thing for about a week. I had made the mistake of taking her down to Marseille for the pleasure of showing her off like a pet puppy to my envious girl friends there. But I got over her in a hurry. She would wake up at four in the afternoon, when I got home from school, lie in bed coloring coloring-books, spend two hours on her wonderful makeup, and then we would drag around Marseille all night, a very uneventful night that immediately made her homesick for Pigalle, her home sweet home. Her strictly vegetative way of life was equaled by her unbelievable ignorance. Beside her, the little French mistress of ceremonies in Rome had been Pico della Mirandola. She was truly a poisonous flower of the night, beautiful and odorless. She knew nothing and had opinions about everything. I no sooner opened my mouth than she stopped me with a tone that brooked no contradiction: "Shut up, you're too fuckin' stupid. You don't know a thing . . ."

Guy, who was in Paris on business, phoned to ask me, "Are you sure that person with you is a girl?"

"Of course."

"Well, watch your step. I've been told he's really a transvestite."

"Look, I can still tell a real woman from a drag queen, even if he were a transsexual!"

Finally, after an endless month, I took advantage of a long weekend to drive her back to Paris. Enough!

Fortunately, in Paris, there was always Geneviève to see, and Sacha Briquet, and wonderful evenings to spend at the home of Boris and Ursula Vian, with Pierre Kast, Marcel Pagliero, Roger and Elisabeth Vailland. We would eat at their dollhouse apartment, where the TV set was placed upside down because Boris said it was "less of a fucking bore than right side up."

In nice weather, we stayed on their huge terrace, which actually was the roof of the Moulin Rouge that they shared with Jacques Prévert, their next-door neighbor. Peter Townsend, Françoise Prévost, and Yannick and Loleh Bellon would come in. We had dazzling conversations till dawn, broken only by servings of fried potatoes and sausages that we went to pick up at the all-night eateries in Place Pigalle.

I was fortunate I had this friendship, with its intelligence, for otherwise my heart would have been terribly empty that year.

Summer came again. From time to time I saw Marie-Laure d'H., who would send me plane tickets so I could spend a weekend in Paris. But then I stayed with her as little as possible, alleging all kinds of obligations, preferring by far to be up on top of the Moulin Rouge than down in the Faubourg Saint-Honoré. Her desperate snobbery just amused me. She was an absolute caricature of Marie-Chantal, that Everyfrenchwoman of the ladies' magazines. She dragged me along like a gigolo to fashionable restaurants and clubs, to boring parties on fancy Avenue Foch or Avenue Henri-Martin. After which I needed the air at Pierre Kast's or Boris's, so as to imbibe some intelligence, humor, and simplicity again.

Marie-Laure was as little lesbian as possible. She liked neither women nor her own body, and lovemaking was always restricted to a few brief twitches during which she gave vent to her mouse's squeak. Her "inversion" was just another bit of snobbery, which she seemed to think added a touch of spice to her fashionable image. But anyway, through her largess, I was able to get up to Paris often that winter. Thanks be to her!

Again I spent the summer at Saint-Tropez, where I went with her, in the huge red-and-white American car that she drove horribly. But I was cautious, so I had rented a little apartment with my pal Nicky, the schoolteacher, in order to keep my independence.

It was a wonderful idyllic summer. Ursula and Boris had come down to their little apartment at La Ponche. Pierre Kast was there, Geneviève and Sacha too. These were heavenly days. At L'Escalet, in the deserted inlets, we girls would lie naked in the sun while the men argued, swam, built new landscapes out of flotsam and rocks salvaged from the sand. Boris was already bothered with his heart trouble. He came to join us only in the afternoons, but as soon as he got there the fun and games took on a different aspect. We shot improvised film stories that went from pirate raids to slave markets to South Sea Island dances, and I still feel sad when I look at the comical photos of that beautiful summer.

Pierre Kast did a film about it, *Le Bel Age,* but I didn't get to play myself in it, because my teaching duties kept me in Marseille.

Then I met two girls who had been living together for

three years. When they both started coming on to me at once, I was ill at ease. But Octavia was a ravishing slim little page, with immense eyes and so much charm and sweetness that I couldn't hold out. However, I don't like to come between a couple, I don't like breaking things up; yet Octavia was too much of a temptation. She was one—at last—who made love wonderfully.

I was living near the Musée de l'Annonciade, she near the church. At dawn, while her friend was still asleep, Octavia would slip out silently to come to me. I woke up sensing her beside me, cool, her bonnet moist with dew and the spray of the port, carrying a flower or a sprig of green she had picked for me.

We made love to each other wildly, frantically, and she would leave me at eight, before her friend was awake. The latter, I like to believe, never suspected a thing. Or, if she did, she was smart enough not to let on. For at the end of the summer our interlude was filed away as just another summer love, and their life together resumed its established course.

So tolerant an attitude is rare among lesbians. In general, we are too possessive to be able to close our eyes to strayings from the path. Female couples don't last as long as male couples, for infidelity with us is almost always followed by separation. There are very few "cuckolds" among us. We are rarely driven by mere physical desire, as men are. We put some sentiment into the slightest liaison and the affair therefore often assumes proportions too great for it to remain unnoticed.

So we are accused of flightiness. It is true that our loves, as a rule, don't last a lifetime. Women are by nature jealous and possessive, which makes compromises difficult, and they usually lead to separation.

Is this good, or is it bad?

Two women who love each other and decide to live together are not held together by anything tangible: not by law, nor by marriage contracts, nor by children, nor by apartment leases. The day when love dies, they are free to split up without restraint. Isn't that preferable to the Calvary of unhappily married couples, bound to the same chain, with nothing left between them but impotent hatred which, as time goes by, becomes total indifference?

Our loves, thank God, are not everlasting, and when we do separate, nothing remains of them: neither torn children nor lawsuits to be settled. Just some scratches and the taste of ashes, as with all human beings. But we are still ready, once the wounds are dressed, to start in again on the wonderful adventure of love, without strings, without mortgages on our future unions.

"The more you make love, the more you will keep on wanting to make it."

That goes for the heart, too: the louder and stronger you make it beat for a new love, the younger it will remain and the better able to keep beating. What a horror when the heart and the ability to love become ossified!

And, anyway, how could anyone be so conceited as to think she could satisfy another for a whole lifetime? How can one be so devoid of imagination and of love for love as to be content with just one being throughout her whole life? What woman can give you *all*, bring you *all*, make you experience *all*?

The point is not to change partners every other day, not to flutter from embrace to embrace in order to "score," but to recognize that the way the human heart is made it can beat several different times, and that it's better that way.

Since more and more young straight couples no longer automatically get married but live together freely, how long do these common-law combinations stay together, when they have no children?

Of course, there are lesbian couples as solidly united as any others. Hundreds of women have lived together for ten, twenty, thirty years. If I am not familiar with them, it is because, among us as elsewhere, happy people don't make news.

The most striking example of that is what I refer to as the "Elephants' Graveyard," that little village near Cannes which has turned into the refuge for couples of superannuated lesbians. They come there to live out their last days. In the little streets, one can see them, leaning on one another's arms, going to call on each other for tea. One finds they have lived together twenty or thirty years. They met when they were around fifty, at the time the senses and the heart begin to simmer down. And if I shiver a bit on seeing them, it is only because I suddenly feel I am getting a glimpse of myself in the maddening mirror of the future.

And there was Aïa, beautiful and titillating, a dancer on her way to Dakar. She gave me a story of her life that was right out of the Arabian Nights' Entertainments, with King Farouk mixed in with the curse of the pyramids and Coptic treasures that her father, a high priest, had defended with his life. She went her way, an evanescent odalisque, and wrote me several passionate letters in phonetic spelling that would have delighted Raymond Queneau. Then nothing more. I got worried, and asked several steward friends to try to find out about her. I discovered she was an "upstairs girl" in a bar in Dakar, that is, one of the whores who take their tricks to the rooms above stairs, and the story of her life and her dancing career was just one more fiction. That hurt me, I felt I had been had. I can't get used to compulsive liars, and mendacity drives me crazy.

And yet there are probably more chronic liars among inverts than in any other group. Perhaps because, by force of circumstance, they are obliged to hide a part of their lives from their families and society. So they have to lie, even if they don't feel like it. Perhaps the more insecure among them one day become unable to recognize the point at which the lies, no longer necessary, have become superfluous.

And there was Monique, an airline hostess with whom I spent one of my most beautiful nights of love. And one of the longest. After such a night, I could easily have fallen in love with her, for my heart almost always follows my body. But Monique was bisexual. That word was not yet fashionable fifteen years ago, when people still said "ambidextrous" or even "AC/DC."

For myself personally I could never fancy women who swing both ways. I have too great an aversion for men to accept them even through the intermediary of a joint partner. The idea that the woman I am holding in my arms could have climaxed with a man a few hours earlier disgusts me, turns off every bit of my desire.

Monique was so boylike, aggressive, conquering, daring, that it was hard to imagine she could have let herself be fucked by a man. I tried not to think of that, but she made a point of it, wanting to cure me of the error of my ways. I had to sleep with men, because that was normal. Sometimes, when she was making love to me, she would suddenly stop, kneeling against my thigh, looking at my body with a rueful air, saying, "Too bad that you won't sleep with a man. What a waste!"

In a word, jam for the sows . . . To hear a woman go over to the other side, to the point of deploring that you would give yourself only to women like her . . . Tough!

After several stopovers between flights, she finally told me that in Tokyo she had met another air hostess who was "normal," that is, who swung both ways, the way she herself did, and that it was all over between us, because my "abnormality" was really too much for her to stomach.

It hurt deeply. In my heart and in my convictions. A lesbian was holding my exclusive homosexuality against me, wanting to make me feel guilty for what was my pride and my reason for living. There are, to be sure, hypocrites who like sleeping with men but cover up with physiological rationalizations: it's necessary for the proper balance of the hormones, or glandular functioning, for the thyroid, the thymus, the kidneys, the spleen, or the balls that we don't have. The vagina, the uterus need to be irrigated, and the best thing there is for watering our flowers is the human garden hose.

But Monique didn't resort to any of those jokes or phony excuses. She slept with men because she liked it, because, having heard somewhere that "if a thing's worth doing, it's worth doing well," she believed in trying everything and carrying it to the point of fulfillment.

I could never fault her really, she was sincere. But I long resented her acting like a recruiting sergeant for the enemy forces.

I left for Brussels to see the World's Fair, as a guest of two stripper-dancers who lived together and put on one of those sado-lesbian acts that were just coming into existence but already had become so highly popular. They had been appearing at the Elle et Lui [Her and Him] for several months.

The Brussels lesbian club where I spent my first evening was a dive. The girls there were lousy, overweight, truck-driver types, the kind one all too often finds in such joints.

One evening the butch of the dancing couple and I were out alone together, when in came a fiery brunette who looked so much like Maïna that it hurt. She was with three men who were dancing attendance on her, each trying to outdo the others. My sidekick and I decided to cruise her. She was a voluptuous, provocative dancer. She came from Calabria and ran a pizzeria near the Bourse.

Getting Maria away from her swains was child's play. This was her first excursion among our tribe and she had an anthropologist's curiosity.

We went up to her place, the three of us, for we had decided we would both make love to her. It was the first time

I'd been in on this kind of setup and I thought it would be fun to try.

We slowly undress her, caressing and kissing her the while. She is hot, ardent, tingling. It promises to be good. My friend kisses her and caresses her breasts. I go down toward the source of all pleasures and set about kissing it. She starts to moan, and I feel her fingers tensing in my hair. I raise my head only long enough to see my pal putting her clothes back on, obviously sore at me, I don't know why. So I close my eyes and finish making love to Maria.

What had happened? Perhaps this was not the right way to make three-way love? I don't know and probably never will, but that doesn't matter at all. There are enough wonders to be discovered in a twosome so that to me counting up to three is a useless exercise. Lesbian group orgies are extremely rare, whereas such things are rather frequent among gay men. Our hearts get mixed in with our bodies, our respect for woman makes it impossible for us to look upon one of our kind as a mere spice, a condiment, a living dildo.

I moved in with Maria. She was widowed and lived with her two children, three younger brothers, and *la mamma*, above the pizzeria. The place was a madhouse, bohemia, filth, noise, Southern Italy in the purest neo-realistic style.

Maria was as jealous and violent as a Calabrian highwayman. She kept me locked up, wouldn't let me go out, wouldn't let me see my friends outside the dark, sordid, and often empty pizzeria. In public, she was haughty, tough, abrasive, and the minute we were alone she started lovemaking with fury, desperately, ending by sobbing on my shoulder as she assured me she loved me. She had driven off all her suitors, and her business was showing it. Those who still turned up looked upon me with murderous vendetta eyes.

How to get away from this petty tyrant, escape from this tigress without creating a scandal? She would never let me go. I finally succeeded in phoning my mother secretly and asking her to send me a wire saying my grandfather (whom

I had never known) had died. I packed my bags, leaving a few things behind as an earnest of my planning to come back. But I'm still running.

Back in Marseille, I met Gisou. A little twenty-year-old nurse's aide, rather cute, with a horrible Marseillais accent, great self-assurance, and very little gray matter. She was free, as was I. She made love very, very well, she had been well schooled in it. And as I was not in love with her, I could indulge in very relaxed lovemaking, without shame or restraint, since I did not have to worry about whether I shocked or displeased her.

I threw myself into a debauch of the senses. Gisou lived with an uncle and aunt who had raised her after her parents died. She had another uncle, a bachelor, who lived with them and fell in love with me. What to do? I couldn't tell him off by showing my hand. I had to pretend to be faithful to my husband and above reproach or temptation. But the uncle still liked to squeeze me into corners, furtively caress my hand, and make calf's eyes at me. I tried to spend as little time as possible at their place, because this male lust, which I was unable to turn away, simply exasperated me.

Gisou told her family that she went out with Guy, me, and a whole gang of nonexistent friends, especially one Jean, a lawyer, whom she made up out of whole cloth to be her "steady."

We stayed together for almost a year. No emotional attachment on my part—far from it. Her lack of culture, her typically Marseillais almost Levantine kind of scheming, rubbed me the wrong way very often, but her nice qualities, her submissiveness, and especially her know-how in lovemaking helped me overlook all the rest.

Gisou showered me with presents out of all proportion to her salary as a nurse's aide. She told me the patients at the private hospital where she worked tipped very handsomely and that besides she had fantastic luck at the races.

But then soon she started getting fat, especially rounding out in the belly, to a very visible degree.

"Well, I'll be darned, you're pregnant," I laughingly told her.

"Not at all," she countered. "My appendix is pressing on my ovaries, and I'm not getting my periods. That's why I'm swelling up. I'm going to have to have my appendix out."

But with each passing day, she got bigger. She flew off the handle when her family suggested she was pregnant. She told them that, working at the clinic, she was well placed to get an abortion if that happened to her, and that she wouldn't have been so stupid as to let it go this long. That made sense.

But the fact that she was urgently in need of an operation was beyond doubt. She went into the clinic as a patient, was operated on, and the next day was almost in a coma, screaming with pain, and no less swollen than before.

As I was waiting in the corridor while they cleaned her up, for she had vomited all over the place, a sweaty, pot-bellied, fiftyish man came along carrying a bouquet of flowers. He was here to see Gisou.

"You understand," he told me, "I'm her friend."

"Well, I'm a friend of hers, too."

"Yes, but I am *her friend*. I'm the one who keeps her."

I thought I had misunderstood. I questioned him further. And learned the horror and sordidness of it. He was in love with Gisou, and she was cheating on him with all the patients in the clinic. He put up with that because she kept assuring him that he was the only one who mattered. He gave her all the money he could; he was only a foreman for the French Electricity Company, and Gisou had expensive tastes. So she went right on cheating on him with the patients and that made him really unhappy. Since I was one of her friends, couldn't I maybe talk to her a little, get her to straighten out?

I was drowned in disgust. My mouth was bitter, I wanted to kill her, to scream with rage and fury.

When Guy got home for dinner he found me sobbing,

trembling with fever. I told him the whole story. Obviously, she was pregnant. I had been sleeping with a whore for months, and all the gifts she had been giving me had been paid for with her heterosexual favors. All those men, all that semen, and here I had been making love to her every night . . . I was yelling at Guy that all women were bitches, liars, sluts, whores. My episode with Monique, the two-way air hostess, was still very recent. I was bleeding at all ends.

I sobbed in Guy's arms.

"Sleep with me, please," I begged him. "I want to be just as whorish as the rest of them. What good is it for me to stay pure, to police my conduct? I'm sick and tired of being considered abnormal, being called an idiot, being insulted this way. Make love to me."

Guy took me in his arms, hugged me very hard, gave me a sleeping tablet with a glass of water, and said, "If I did that, you'd hate yourself in the morning. And turn on me, to boot. Sleep. I love you, and you, for one, are not a whore."

The next day I went to the clinic. Gisou was giving birth to a preemie. She was screaming as loud as she did when we made love. The same animal cries. I stayed there on purpose, my forehead pressed against the window, nails digging into the palms of my hands. I clenched my teeth so as not to scream out my rage, my disgust, my scorn. I stayed there to punish myself for my credulity, to expiate my naiveté, hoping I would hear her die. I was weeping with hate. When it was all over, and the placenta had been carried away in a basin, I went near the bed where Gisou lay livid, sweating, exhausted, slapped her and called her a whore, and then walked out.

The whore's child lived for two hours.

But that wasn't the end of the story. Gisou's family, once the danger was over—for the idiot had come damn close to dying—demanded an explanation. And since she allegedly had been going out only with me and Guy and our friends, they wanted me to tell them who the father was. I felt they suspected Guy. Or could it have been Jean, that lawyer she had made up? I gave my word that it couldn't be either one of them.

I filled them in on the fat guy from the day before and all he had told me. I had his address. He had to be the father. Gisou's uncle and I went over to his place. The uncle punched him a couple of times and the big soft mass of lard started to bawl and ask what we wanted of him.

"You slept with my niece, you bastard, and she's just miscarried. You'll pay for this, through the nose!"

"But I wasn't the only one. It could have been a pile of others."

The taste of bile, of vomit welled back into my mouth. I had slept with the bitch. She had lain under this fat sack that stunk with fear. And all just for me, just so she could shower me with presents and try to dazzle me, to hang on to me by spoiling me. What a cunt! My God, what a stupid cunt!

In the meantime, old fatty was trying to wriggle out of it, quibbling about dates. He seemed relieved to find out she had been six months pregnant.

"Then it can't be me. It's not me. You can check with the Electricity Company. Six months ago, I spent six weeks at the plant near Grenoble, without ever coming back to Marseille."

Sick of him by now, the uncle and I left him alone. He had been punched, insulted; we had gotten some of it out of our systems. We threatened him every which way should he ever dare try to see her again, and I spat in his face as we went away.

There's no need for me to say that even though I continued to see her for her family's sake, there was no question of my touching her. As soon as we were alone together I would insult her, rehash all my fury again, tongue-lash her, blast her with all the vilest terms, the most scornful, the lewdest I could think of. Carried away by my anger, provoked by her stubborn silence, I finally slapped her, pushed her around. She let me, her little angel face closed, determined, silent. And she stayed on. And she came back, telling me she loved me, expecting God knows what, like a faithful dog.

Finally, her relatives shipped her off to Bordeaux to another uncle, so I was at last shed of them, especially that free-feeling uncle.

Then I met Valérie, who was nineteen, frail, and long, and who also reminded me of Maïna; Maïna, after whom there had been no other real love. There had been passions, passing affairs, but not real love. Valérie the unsettling, with baby's breasts, doe's eyes, and a perfect face.

Valérie was nothing, really, just a soap bubble. So young, so naive, I scarcely dared go near the little Tanagra. And, besides, she was under age; when I found out she had left her home and that her family was looking for her, I immediately stopped seeing her.

One-night lovers I had aplenty and more. I didn't care for that. I wanted to "settle down." I wanted to live with a woman I loved.

Pierre Kast one day had said to me, speaking of my latest friend, "How is your herbarium coming along?" I had thought it was a cute idea and had gotten a looseleaf leather album and had *Herbarium* and my initials inscribed on the cover. I tried to paste in pictures of all my ladies, with little descriptive records of them. It was horrible, and in very bad taste, to be sure, but it had been a lot of fun. No one had ever seen it. I wasn't cynic enough for that, but I had talked about it a lot. So much so that one evening in Marseille's Classic Club, as I was having a conversation with a girl who seemed to have attracted me, the owner came close and whispered in my ear, "Not worthy of your herbarium."

The worst part was that I had just been having exactly the same thought. I had felt, hard up as I was, that I might sleep with her, but the idea of having to put her into my herbarium album gave me pause. That was how fatuous, pretentious, and confoundedly cynical I had become. It had to stop; I had to live a dutiful, settled, bourgeois life; I suddenly realized that was what I so terribly missed.

CHAPTER

V

I MET DOMINIQUE AT THE TROIS FONTAINES. SHE WAS A BIG girl with regular Greek-statue features, a serious, reserved air about her. I struck up a conversation with her at the bar. She seemed sweet, intelligent, lively. We spent an agreeable evening talking a great deal and dancing very little. She was not at all the type that usually attracts me, the child-woman younger than I, beautiful but birdbrained, whom I can dominate and protect, teach about life, love, and suffering. She was thirty, my age. She was an equal, a peer, and my feeling for her was mainly one of empathy.

The next day I returned to Marseille. She seduced me through her letters, the way they were written, what they said. At last, here was a sensitive, cultivated, intelligent woman. She worked as a tax collector, adored classical music, had never had sex with a man, loved the country, open fireplaces, and the books of Montherlant.

When I was back in Paris a month later, I called her without losing a moment.

"Enough of all this talk," I said, "let's get down to business. It's tonight or never. How about dinner?"

I feared that our epistolary relationship, our mutuality of tastes, might lead simply to a friendship. I felt she was shy, shyer even than I, so I had to be forward. I was thirty, old already as I saw it, the best years of my life behind me. I really had to settle down, preferably with the right kind of girl, almost contract a marriage of convenience. It was getting pretty late . . .

Passion and frenzy were a discovery to her, and the way they dazzled her made her even dearer to me.

"One diamond polishes another, one woman refines another, leaving her gentle, tempered," said the Duc de Morny. Dominique and I represented harmony, communion.

But she was living in Paris and I in Marseille. Very soon, we couldn't stand the constant separations any longer. We were on Cloud Nine when we were together, of course, but there were all those empty weeks in between. We considered the alternatives: I could move to Paris; but in Marseille I had a very nice apartment, and there was the seashore and the sunlight. Paris meant gray skies, looking for an apartment, and besides—would Guy be happy if I were to leave him?

After a year of this, Dominique told her mother, with whom she lived, that if it was all right with her, she was going to put in for a transfer to Marseille. Her father had died a few months before we met and since then her mother had been going from one depression to another. But now she seemed much better and she approved of her daughter's suggestion. Leaving Paris was the very best thing to do. Elula, her best friend, lived in the South, and besides, Dominique and her mother owned some land down there. A splendid idea.

A few weeks later, she went into another depression. Dominique went down to the garage to get the car and take her mother to the hospital. When she got downstairs, the horrified concierge greeted her with the news that her mother had just jumped from the sixth story.

By that evening, I was in Paris with her.

I felt a little bit at fault in this. If she had not met me, if I had been willing to move to Paris, if she had not decided to come to the Midi, if this, if that . . .

Now more than ever, it was imperative for her to come

to Marseille. There was nothing to keep her now; quite the contrary. The apartment had become unbearable, her memories too painful.

Dominique was a civil servant, and getting transferred to the South was just about impossible. Had I lived in Nancy or Arras, no sweat, but positions in the sun belt were at a premium. The only answer was to marry a man from Marseille, so that Dominique might be given priority in order to be able to be with her husband.

I knew a few local gays, particularly two navigators who lived together, simple, understanding fellows. Gérard was quite amenable to marrying Dominique. In no more time than it took to fill out the necessary papers, this "fabricated" marriage was under way.

It was not a fancy wedding, no beribboned limousines, no bridesmaids or wedding gowns, but just the family: his parents, and her aunt and uncle, his friend and me. After the ceremony, performed by the mayor of a Marseille suburb, we had drinks at the home of the parents of the "groom." They were simple working people who lived in a tiny two-rooms-and-kitchen apartment. Dominique's aunt and uncle were rather put out. They were afraid she had married beneath her; the boy was good-looking enough, and quite impressive, but his accent was so lower-class Southern . . . However, they probably thought, Dominique was a big girl now, all alone in life, and if this was what she wanted, down in Marseille, so be it. Besides, there was always good old Elula, such a nice friend, who had been such a comfort after her mother died.

It was all over in an hour. In order to go back to town, we all had to pile into my Dauphine, Uncle, Auntie, the bride and the groom, with his best man sitting on his lap!

We drove the relatives back to the railroad station and then hotfooted it to Le Corbusier to lock ourselves up for a week. The bride and groom, of course, were supposed to have gone on a honeymoon, which, to be sure, they had no intention of doing. Gérard and Roger occupied one bedroom, Dominique and I the other. I was the only one who went out, just to bring back food and supplies.

It was a delightful week, and postcards were obligingly sent from Rome by some girls we had made arrangements with. Later, Gérard was to make a perfect fool of himself: He got the idea I was jealous of his having married Dominique! He started shooting his mouth off, creating all kinds of impossible situations, and we just had to stop seeing him.

Dominique and he are still legally married. They write each other at New Year's or when one of them needs the other's signature on something. Anyway, I don't know of any lesbian–gay man marriage that has ever worked out, whereas most straight people think that a woman and man who are both gay would pair off marvelously.

That is a misconception. On the sexual scale, we're at opposite extremes. The male homosexual only wants to tell us about his latest conquest's big cock, going into utmost detail about its length and thickness. We certainly can't come back with the depth, tightness, or degree of hygrometry of our girl friend's vagina, because we don't discuss that kind of thing. Male inverts are almost all oversexed, they always have men on their minds.

The lesbians and gay men who get along well together are really the great exceptions. More often, they're like fellow convicts, both groups being socially banned and ostracized. As with all minorities, they flock together so as to feel less alone. In the provinces, lesbians are welcomed in gay men's bars because they add to the numbers, but in Paris the mixture is less common, each group staying within its own preserve.

Straight women are often quite happy around gay men, because they are charming escorts who surround them with an inoffensive and sterile kind of courtship that their husbands know represents no threat to them.

But we don't want male courtship, whether from gays or straights. And the women who make a habit of cottoning to gay men, "fairy godmothers" or "fag hags," as they are often called, are actually overage straights who secretly hope they can still score with one of their youthful companions, some night when he's alone or has had a fight with his lover.

Marriages between inverts of opposite sexes are almost always fiascoes. These unconsummated nuptials entered into just to pacify families or to act as cover for some situation, turn sour once the bride and groom are alone under the same roof.

If the "husband" is the faithful type, his lover will not readily accept having a woman share his darling's name. He will feel frustrated, throw fits of jealousy, create an atmosphere of tension, and it'll end in divorce. The same thing happens if the "bride" has a steady lover.

If the gay male has short, multiple affairs, as so often happens, he will be bringing home to the "conjugal nest" whatever he cruises in a bar, a men's room, or a public urinal. The house will no longer be a home, but more like a railway station waiting room. The fly-by-nights will steal everything in sight, whether records or T-shirts, not to mention those long-distance calls to Cannes or New York. The lesbian won't stand for it. She'll lock herself in her room.

The whole place will reek of male presence, and it will turn her stomach. Men writers have sung the glories of the *odore di femmina*, which I certainly would be the last to decry, but there is also a stench of male, heavy, invading, and in any case "different." We in the West may consider blacks and Orientals to have a strong, offensive odor, but in Vietnam it is the whites who are said to exude the horrible musty and sweetish odor of corpses.

Soon the spouse of the fickle gay man won't be able to put up with it, and once again the bittersweet verbal blasts will lead to the divorce court.

To my personal knowledge, no such marriage has ever lasted more than a year. Cohabitation of the two castes just does not work.

It does happen, however, that the two partners get married specifically so as to have a child, even though they have agreed to remain free each to have her/his own separate life-style.

In this kind of case, too, it rarely lasts. One of the two gets to be jealous and resents the other's inversion.

No, it is much better for an inverted woman who wants to get married, and especially one who wants to have a child, to marry a straight male, with the situation well established between them in advance. The husband will be free to "cheat" on his wife as often as he wants, while she entertains all the girls she feels like, and the husband will only be the happier for it: being surrounded by two or three women, though they may not be his to take, will appeal to the pasha in him, delighting him with the illusions of a harem atmosphere.

But I am hard put to understand the utter need to get married that seems to haunt some lesbians. Is it really worth going to all that trouble just to pacify one's family? I don't know of any bloody tragedies brought on by the discovery that we are "like that." Granted, not all girls are so lucky as to have a mother as tolerant and understanding as mine, with her Oriental fatalism. But after a longer or shorter period of revolt, indignation, and fury, the family finally comes around. In the final analysis, the current steady is even recognized by her "in-laws." The mother, especially, will establish secret bonds of complicity with her. She feels she has gained a second daughter, rather than having lost her own, as so often happens when a girl marries.

We are often accused of being ashamed of our inversion. But it is not shame that we are showing. It is love and respect for our parents. The lesbian doesn't want to make her life-style known, for fear it will make them unhappy. Marriages of convenience or cover marriages can most often be accounted for on that basis alone.

Once married, Dominique was quickly transferred to the Internal Revenue Service in Marseille. She sold her Paris apartment and bought a studio at Le Corbusier, which she promptly sublet, since naturally we were going to live together and have a settled, peaceful life—just what I had so wished for.

She taught me to appreciate classical music, which I was not very familiar with, and we read wonderful books together.

She owned an old run-down house surrounded by olive trees, two hours out of Marseille, at the foot of Mont Ventoux. We fixed it up over the years, almost entirely with our own hands. And in that picturesque little village this daughter of the Indochinese rice paddies discovered the French countryside. From Dominique's childhood friends, farmers all, I learned about the earth with its four seasons, picked cherries, gathered strawberries, plucked lime-blossom leaves, dug up potatoes, made hay, harvested grapes, and came full circle with the picking of the olives.

We went to the mountains in the winter, to the beach in summer, to Paris a couple of times a year to see friends, go to the theater, take in the art galleries. This was the life I had dreamed of, life as I wanted it to be.

Dominique had rented her unused studio to a very engaging sixty-year-old businessman, who quickly understood what we were and often asked us in for a drink in what he had turned into his bachelor digs.

One day he got up the courage to show us his collection of dildoes—which we in French call *godemichés*, from the Latin *gaude mihi*, meaning "pleasure me." And was I ever pleasured! I had never had a chance to see any, certainly not such a variety, fat ones, medium ones, ones with squirt bulbs, with suction cups at the end (so they could be attached to a wall for self-service!), some decorated with flower petals, or bristly at the end like a pine cone, and more. What a selection! What imagination, what a wonderworld of tools!

As might be expected, all this belonged to a man who used it to supplement his own virility, not always up to satisfying the youthful partners he lured to his place.

For lesbians very rarely resort to such contraptions, in spite of certain myths. Why in the world would we want to adorn ourselves with such ersatz monstrosities?

It all comes back to that short innervation of the vagina, and the resulting uselessness of such phalluses, whether real or simulated.

Could anyone think they look good? The belts that hold them on are exciting only if you get turned on by hernial trusses.

So? The few lesbians who sport them are either sorry transsexual "butches" or cabaret hookers who make use of them to accommodate their male or female tricks. Unfortunately for the new women-men, while it is possible surgically to create vaginas as artificial as the paradises of the same name, no one has yet found a way to graft in those couple of inches of crucial flesh they would so like to acquire. The day they do, what a fantastic market in transsexuation there will be, what an open season for sex options!

"I'll swap you my penis for your clitoris, and we can switch IDs . . ."

But since almost all the drag queens who have the operation become lesbians, at that time maybe the rebuilt men-women would turn out to be gay boys.

There really is nothing paradoxical about coming to such a conclusion. The men who undergo this operation have always felt themselves to be so feminine, have so hated what they had dangling from their crotches, that once they are turned into pseudowomen their aversion for the male sex gets the better of them and they now seek refuge in the arms of other women, their sisters whom they had so long wanted to be like. I've often met couples of this kind in which the femme was the one who had been born a boy and the boyish natural-born girl was the butch of the household.

Guy hadn't been sharing the place with me for quite some time now. I had introduced him to Gina and they were now living together.

One of my fellow teachers had introduced me to her. Gina was thirty-five, had three daughters, a husband who was an architect, and lovers galore. She was quite beautiful, although plump. She had grown tired of men and now wanted to try lovemaking on the other side of the Rubicon in order to find out whether it was equally dull.

She didn't appeal to me physically, but we liked each other. Then one day she met Guy. Love at first sight. In the beginning, she would take my hands, kiss them, kneel down before me and say in a tiny trembling and earnest voice, "Thanks for lending Guy to me. What happiness you've given me . . ."

Embarrassed, I made her get up. It was really all too melodramatic!

"I'm not lending you anything," I said. "You know very well that Guy is entirely free."

But she quickly got over her bedazzlement. She came to with a brutal start and hated me as frenetically as she had adored me. Notwithstanding Guy's advice, she had gotten a divorce, and now that she was free she couldn't understand why he wouldn't get one too and marry her.

He wasn't anxious to. The setup suited him very well. His little attraction for her had quickly worn itself out when she started in with her fits of jealousy and threats of suicide. But since he was a weakling, he stayed with her, for fear of what she threatened to reveal to his parents, and perhaps, too, because it was rather flattering to him to be adored with such passion. For, while Guy's career had prospered brilliantly, the personal life I had given him was in no way ideal . . . We now got together once or twice a week to go and have lunch at his parents'. Soon not only Gina was objecting to this, but Dominique as well!

After a year or so, almost every week I had to put up with a scene from her after I had seen my nominal husband. It was painful, stupid, unbearable, and without justification. Dominique was jealous of the degree of security my marriage afforded me. I could always count on Guy if things got tough, and financially he was a big help. Money—what a stumbling-block to sex! How many women, lesbians though they be, have to suffer the tail between men's thighs if they are to acquire some degree of material ease! How can one support a lesbian life-style on a secretary's or a salesgirl's salary?

My friends and I may very well kiss our girl friends' hands at such fancy restaurants as Lasserre's or Castel's without worrying about snide comments or sneers. In the cheaper places with paper tablecloths where it takes a nimble elbow to keep from rubbing the butter off a neighbor's radish, Sapphic poetry hardly dares to rear its head. Only fine tablecloths, chandeliers, and separate tables with decent spaces between them allow us to feel we are not the target of eavesdropping eyes and ears.

Money is all well and good, but since men are generally the ones who have it, in a certain way they still have a hold over us, even when we try to get out of their grasp.

Guy was willing to give me anything without asking for any payoff, and the girls found this hard to believe and accept. My union with Maïna had run aground in part because of her jealousy, and now Dominique's was taking the same turn. But all that Guy and I did when we were together was to talk about stock-market quotations, politics, business projects—in a word, the things that his life was made up of.

After each of these luncheons, Dominique harassed me with leading questions. Her outbursts of jealousy over Guy became more and more frequent. He and I, in order to spare ourselves the ordeal in our respective households, now had to meet secretly, on the sly, in out-of-the-way assignation spots, as if we were clandestine lovers. It was ludicrous.

Gina had me tailed for several months by a private eye. She hoped to discover a man in my life, so she could prove to Guy that I was playing him for a sucker. Because she knew that was the only thing I might do that he would never forgive. He had always said, "If I ever find out you're sleeping with another man, I'll rape you."

"You'd be right," I told him. "If I did want a man, why wouldn't I come to the sweetest, most wonderful one there is?"

Gina finally decided that I was the one who was unwilling to give Guy a divorce, and suggested to him that he buy me off so he might be free. She had lots of money, and she believed everything in life could be bought if you were only willing to pay the price.

The atmosphere Guy and I were living in had become a plague.

Dominique cheated on me with a fat broad. I am not intuitive at all, but rather trusting and credulous, so some "well-meaning friends" had to open my eyes for me. I was furious. This couldn't even be rationalized: being dropped for someone more attractive than I might make sense, but not this!

For a few weeks I insulted her, made life a hell for her, compared her to Gisou and called her a whore, she who had never slept with a man in her whole life and had had so very brief and dull a love life before meeting me . . .

At a party given by my pal Jacky, the schoolmistress, we met a little girl with a shock of black hair and splendid green eyes, a laboratory technician at the medical school. Her name was Catherine and she and Jacky occasionally made it together. She and I hit it off, so I asked her over the next time I had a dinner, thinking I'd pair her up with a little blonde from Salon-de-Provence who had been coming on to me without getting anywhere.

I loved Dominique, we were a happy couple. Besides, I have

the soul of a matchmaker, so I figured that the pretty little blonde and the pretty little brunette would make a pretty little pair.

After dinner, we all went to the Paradou, a gay bar near the Opéra. But nothing lit up between the two of them.

When I asked Catherine what she'd drink, and she said pineapple juice, I didn't even hear her. All I saw were her cat's eyes looking at me, and I knew then that I loved her.

We sparred around for a month. We laid our eyes on each other, caressed each other with words. Neither of us was in a hurry.

Her parents were in the *charcuterie* business, which is not exactly glamorous. And they had just sold the shop. So they had nothing left that would appeal to my well-known taste for pork sausages and cold cuts.

Catherine was neither stupid nor vulgar. She had a very acceptable rough polish that merely had to be buffed. Once again I saw that my tastes ran true to form: I was not concerned about my lover's intellect. Dominique had been the exception.

Finally, one afternoon, I called on Catherine at her laboratory. She looked real tiny in her white smock. White smock, hospital, Maïna . . . We kissed between the test tubes and a Geiger counter. She was hot, ardent. We made love a few times at my place, of an afternoon. Like Tristan, she waited for Dominique to go back to work and for me to put a white sheet in the window as a signal.

Right off, we were madly in love, physically passionate. She was twenty-two and I thirty-five, but I didn't show it. And one day, after Dominique had been more ludicrous than ever in berating me about Guy, I exclaimed in exasperation,

"I don't love you anymore. I love someone else."

"Who?" she demanded to know.

"Catherine."

Turning on my heels, I slammed the door behind me and left her in tears, bleeding to death, and flew off cruelly, egotistically, without the slightest remorse, toward my new love.

Dominique rushed to the phone, to look for some support, some consolation, some friendship from—you guessed it!—Guy.

What a joke! After having scorched me for being dependent on him, now she ran to him for help. Soon she would not make a move in the market, not even call her broker, without first getting his approval. And he, being sweet and nice as ever, forgot her past hostility and asked her to lunch so they could talk about me.

I was swimming in happiness. Dominique had moved back into her studio. We had remained on friendly terms. Or almost—for she found it hard to be anything but uncivil toward Catherine.

"Your delicatessen dolly who only knows how to make love and play belote," was the way she sneeringly referred to her.

"Well, since I love to do both, nothing could be better. And at least she doesn't carry on about that husband of mine, whom you suddenly seem to adore!"

I nicknamed Catherine *Le Chat,* or Cat, because of her eyes, her claws, and the way she meowed.

Our love had begun in March, the same month that had brought me Maïna, Dominique, and would later bring me Aimée. In March Moustique had introduced me to Woman. Could it be that the coming of spring every three or four years accounts for such a thorough housecleaning in my heart?

Is it body weariness that makes me available for a new love, or heart weariness? I don't know. The only sure thing about it is that it turns up like a hurricane. The sky may be calm as can be, then out of the blue comes the headlong dash toward a new body, a new sex, a new bosom, new kisses, new harmonies of sighs and cries, the whole intoxicating epic of love that I seem to be discovering afresh each time. So it is never any problem for me to keep from talking to my friends about how my earlier mistresses made love. Intimacy between two beings, even if it lasted only a minute or a day, is something too precious to be spread out in another's sheets.

In that way, too, we women are different from men. While we may suggest that some girl is a "prospect," we rarely go on to recount in detail what we mean.

June finally arrived.

We had had the crazy idea of turning our house at the foot of Mont Ventoux into a little summer restaurant.

I had quit teaching the year before because once more I had felt my headmistress was beginning to be wary of me, and I left without waiting to be fired yet again "without cause." Teaching was over for me. This was one lesbian who would never again be a threat to the future generations of little girls who were sleeping with boys as early as the ninth grade.

So we had set up our dining room to accommodate twenty-one at lunch. I was to do the cooking. I made grilled meats with Provençal herbs (just then coming into fashion) on a little charcoal heater out on the street. A simple menu, vegetables grown by the local farmers, and wine from their own barrels.

The June waitress was to be a lesbian tax colleague of Dominique's who would put in her month's vacation there; in July, a friend who taught phys. ed.; and in August, Dominique.

We had the customary gala opening, inviting the one hundred and twenty locals to be our guests. All of them came—although split up into two separate waves, one made up of the Communists, the other of the Catholics.

We feted them all regally with sparkling wine. They were both amused and proud to have a restaurant in the tiny village since it didn't have another shop of any kind, not even the usual *café-tabac*.

And business boomed! Saturday afternoon at two, Cat would arrive and stay till Monday morning. During the week, once or twice she'd hop into her little Citroën as soon as she got out of the lab, dash down to see me, make love madly, and then leave for Marseille again at one in the morning.

Dominique and she still weren't wild about one another, but both were smart enough to avoid direct confrontations.

The locals as well as the summer people were amazed by the string of girls who came to pitch in at the Petite Auberge.

The day of the annual village fair, there were ten of us waiting table in the restaurant, handling the game booths for the children, drawing the raffle, giving prizes to winners of the *pétanque* bowling contest, and so on. Never had there been fair so fair!

Word spread as far as Carpentras and Cavaillon that there was this inn kept by a bunch of women. Vegetable wholesalers came by in the afternoon. They ordered champagne and then asked what the going rate was. At first we were offended, but later we decided to take it in our stride and turn them away with our fiercest bazookas.

There was lovemaking in the rooms above, to be sure, but only between Cat and me!

One day, I found the toilet seat splattered with semen. One of the gents had really been ready to pop when he came to our place looking for relief. I washed away the traces of his climax and then went and threw up.

Sunday morning we did a land-office business in *pastis*, that legal near-absinthe of the South. The men of the village came in to chat to the accompaniment of Beethoven and Mozart tapes that I played. And they asked for more. *Pastis* time was now a cultural event! In the afternoons, the clientele would be the women and kids. Then we went in more for Piaf and dance tunes. I prepared Vietnamese meals to order, and the whole region learned to eat with chopsticks that summer.

Finally, in mid-August I turned the restaurant over to Dominique and left for Yugoslavia with Cat—our first vacation. For several nights, I kept waking up with the same nightmare: I was back at the Petite Auberge, cooking, preparing, waiting table. What I had thought I enjoyed doing for three months had obviously taken so much out of me that it was now haunting me. I still had a lot to learn about myself. Not to know whether what you are doing appeals to you or not, whether the one you're making love to is the one you love or not . . .

After that vacation, I decided to get a job again. I couldn't remain inactive. I felt useless, like an invalid, compared to all my friends who were working. I answered a want ad and became a pollster for a Parisian outfit. For the next two years, I was to go all over France, alone or as part of a team, with girls who by and large were all very nice. We would come into some town for a week or two, wreak havoc in the hotel where the six to ten of us were lodged, visiting from room to room, having fun, making do at night with a ham sandwich in our bedrooms to economize so as to be able to have fancy lunches in the best little restaurants in the town or near it.

I have very good memories, for example, of one survey we did for the French Radio/Television Service, on Nice in the month of May. From noon to four every afternoon we were on the beach, and then we took off each on our own. Generally, we had to get about a dozen questionnaires filled out each day.

Some of us took half as long as the others, and I was especially lucky. I made a good first impression and almost never got turned away. And a good thing, too, for I couldn't have stuck it if each day I had met with rebuffs, rejections, curses, and doors slammed in my face.

Still, it took all the courage I had to ring a doorbell. I swore to myself at that time that if ever anyone came ringing at my door, I'd cooperate—even with those who were soliciting funds. What a constitution it takes to ring doorbells, it's tough, it's exhausting.

Fortunately, this door-knocking business was the occasion for a lot of funny incidents, and we would tell each other about them before retiring to our respective hotel rooms, which varied in comfort and luxury from town to town and from budget to budget. How distrustful and inhospitable the French were, closeted in their appallingly identical lodgings, with the same prints on the walls, the same mail-order sideboards, the same bad taste, disorder, sloppiness. Working-class, minor executives', petty liberal-professionals' homes, how I hated you during those two door-to-door years, with my frozen smile and my "Good afternoon, madam, I'm not selling anything. We would just like to ask . . ."

And the higher-class, more "bourgeois" homes, that were even harder to get into, with their family furniture, Louis XV living rooms, their dull layouts, their grayness and lack of personality. I drove about through France, and Cat wrote me care of general delivery, where all of us went together every day to pick up our mail. I was married and, therefore, supposed to be getting letters from Guy. My co-workers were amazed to see that he still wrote me so often after so many years of marriage.

It was at this time that I met Thérèse. She managed a cathouse hotel in Rue Thubaneau, the lowest of all the "hot streets" in Marseille. I had met her at a gay joint and been fascinated by her truculence and the raciness of her language.

We became friends.

Thérèse was my age and looked twenty years older. A foundling, she had lived the classic script: housemaid, raped by her employer at fifteen, streetwalking, Caracas, Dakar, whorehouses, Marseille. She had never had a pimp, which made her a notable exception. She was really tough, and smart as a whip. Now, at thirty-six, used up, worn to the bone, she managed this cathouse that was owned by a respectable businesswoman. Thérèse was the front, the straw woman, paying the fines and if need be doing the time for maintenance of an illegal disorderly house. The irreproachable owner came by only once a week to check on the figures. There were four or five girls working out of the place, put there by their macks. They paid five francs per trick for the room and two more for a condom. Each one had her own column in the school notebook in which the accounts were kept. Every time a girl took a john upstairs a line was drawn in her column. So the macks and the landlady could tell the exact number of tricks turned each week.

Often, on Sunday afternoons, we'd go over and play belote with Thérèse. Cat and I would come in, sometimes with Dominique, looking very societyish and carrying a box of pastries with a ribbon on it. I would park as close to the hotel as possible so as to avoid hoots and catcalls from the customers. The girls on the street got to recognize us and if the johns gave us a hard time they'd line up to assure us safe passage to the hotel.

We would embrace Thérèse's girls, pacing their beat at the entrance to the hotel, before we went up the one flight to the "office," which was also Thérèse's living quarters; and there we played cards till evening. Sometimes we'd stay to dinner. Thérèse was a divine cook. The girls sat down with us. We talked. Some were rough and some were bright, but they were all lousy-looking, for this was strictly a grind street.

I remember one Christmas Eve.

The girls knocked off work at nine. We had a late dinner, with all the trimmings: smoked salmon, turkey, Yule log, the thirteen Provençal desserts, champagne. The treat lasted a full hour, then they went back to the grind. From ten till six in the morning, they never stopped tricking. Men were lined up right along the stairways outside the rooms. They didn't even know which one they would get to hump, because there was no time for the girls to go down on the street to make their pickups.

The johns started undressing in the hallways and the tarts turned them out so fast, once their little business had been pulled off, that they often emerged with their pants and jackets over their arms.

Some of the men looked cheeky, and others slunk along

the walls, sheepishly. Some stuck their heads through the "office" wicket to pass the time of night. We were watching midnight mass on TV.

Every time she saw a very young lad come in, Thérèse, who was real thoughtful, would ask,

"Is this your first time, sonny?"

And if the boy answered yes, she'd roar up the stairs: "Josette! Be extra nice! I'm sending you up a cherry!"

She'd make way for him, forcing the other johns to let him go ahead of them. When he came back out, they'd shout congratulations, and the poor kid would scamper off through the uproar. On a Saturday night, a girl would accommodate from seventy to eighty customers. They only washed out every eighth or ninth time, because they couldn't have stood the irritation of that many successive douches. Let us pause to give a tender, compassionate thought to that poor number eight or nine . . .

Average time for "lovemaking" (dressing and undressing included): three minutes and thirty seconds.

There were peepholes into the rooms, so that Thérèse could keep an eye on any customers who seemed suspicious to her. She had been stabbed three times. With her own body thus scarred from the war for survival, she would impress on all the girls the prostitute's golden rule: Never turn your back on a customer.

At first, I used to take an occasional look through the peephole.

It amused me for a while, because I wasn't very well versed in heterosexual play, but to watch that smooth-skinned puppet with its stupid look stand erect and hard for just a flash became so monotonous to me that I was quickly sick of it and after that we left the office only when there was an especially exciting incident.

For instance, to go and look at the five little draftees on the way to camp who had "gone up" with the same girl, and were manually keeping their respective manhoods at the ready while waiting to get their turn to shove it in. If we had told them that they were exhibiting signs of latent homosexuality, they would probably have run away . . .

Or the very young law clerk who always selected the sturdiest girl of the bunch because he had to have her gallop around the room two or three times with him riding piggyback before he could get it up.

Nanou, a hefty peasant girl who had come here straight from her mountain home above Manosque, started yelling in her room one night. Thérèse rushed out, her bull's pizzle in hand, followed by Chanaz, the Algerian maid, who was built like a weightlifter and often acted as interpreter, but more often as bouncer, carrying a nightstick in hers.

They rushed into the room, which was never locked—that being the hooker's second golden rule—and before asking any questions, walloped the half-naked john. Then, Thérèse turned to Nanou to ask what was up, while Chanaz held the man at bay with her weapon.

"What did he do to you?"

"He wants me to suck him off."

"Well, why don't you want to?"

"Because he's a Jew. I don't suck Jews."

He was a young ensign from the Israeli fleet, just as cute as could be.

Finally, after Thérèse told her that in this hotel you either gave the customer what he wanted or refunded his money, she did as she was asked, but she didn't put her heart into it. When the little officer left, he seemed quite satisfied and was all smiles. He must have gone away thinking that in Marseille it was customary to get a few blows along with the blow job.

Very few of the whores were lesbians, in contrast to high-class call girls. For these girls, too, a man becomes nothing more than the (literal) tool of the trade, wholly without romance or attractiveness, but they don't have much time left for playing with each other.

Those poor girls who fifty times a day drag up the sticky

stairs of a dark hallway and spend ten hours a day in a dilapidated hotel room have only one idea at bedtime, and that is to get to sleep alone and not to dream.

They got out once a week, with their "sweet man," who took them to a restaurant, the movies, and home to sleep by midnight. In summer, they got one big outing to Cassis or Bandol. In a word, they were living it up.

Finally, Thérèse got busted and did three months for harboring prostitutes, as she must have expected. When she got out, somebody else had been hired for her job. She had to go back to the life. She wept bitter tears of chagrin and discouragement, because she had been sure that her own whoring days were over. She lived alone with six mutts and two cats, an empty heart, a sagging body, bitter and hostile. Back when she ran the hotel, she had been wildly generous, spending her money openhandedly, treating and entertaining a whole armada of freeloading faggots. When she landed back on her bit of turf, everyone dropped her except for us. I still included her at my dinners. And she met my friends, but they embarrassed her, overawed her, because she was sure they looked down on her, knowing how low she had fallen. Yet it made her so happy. Her language may have been of the gutter, but her heart was very sweet.

One fine day, my friend Thérèse just vanished. I don't know what happened to her. Two or three times I tried to go back to Rue Thubaneau to ask about her, but I had to give up; next to it, the Rue de la Goutte-d'Or is as safe and peaceful as the Rue de la Paix, so one doesn't dare venture on it anymore, even by car.

At one time, Thérèse had almost convinced me that investing in a call hotel was the surest way to make money. Every one of them is owned by very respectable people. If I bought, she would manage. I had just collected my war damages from Indochina, after twenty years, and it seemed like a good idea. We studied the return, I went two or three times to look over some of the hotels on the street with Dominique, decided on one, and even went so far as to put up a binder. But at the last minute, I came to. How could I live on the proceeds of sperm spilt on bed sheets? No way. Money does have an odor. That one turned my stomach and I thought it was better to go on ringing bells and knocking on doors.

When I got back from my polling tours, Cat and I, still in love, still happy, sometimes spent weekends at Aubagne, with Rose, who lived in an isolated farmhouse that had the good smell of furze and rosemary.

I had known Rose for many years and come to visit her with my successive lovers. Despite her feminine name, she was an androgynous creature dressed in a lumber jacket, gym shoes, and beret, whom everyone addressed as Monsieur.

She was the daughter of a leading surgeon of Marseille. He had loved her madly and tried to rape her at fifteen. He offered to set her up in regal style as his mistress, if only she agreed. She didn't. Her mother was an invalid who stayed in bed and never left her room, which she locked at night, without ever a thought to that lost little adolescent, her daughter Rose.

She had done a little studying of some kind and when she was twenty her father had sent her away here, to this huge empty barn. She lived there, raising chickens which almost all died because she never remembered to feed them or to turn the heat on in the incubators.

To be truthful, she drank five or six bottles of red wine per day. She was small, sickly-looking, but had a disconcerting sharpness of mind in her lucid moments.

Rose's place was a way station for every down-on-her-luck lesbian in France. They would tip each other off to the address, like hippies before the fact, and drop in, dirty, haggard, like wandering cats. Rose fed them and housed them for a few days or weeks, and then they moved on, carrying off a trinket or a piece of clothing, or leaving behind a painting or a guitar.

My pal Nicky went there very often. It was a good hunting

preserve for her, and when she found one who wasn't too dirty or too ugly she'd bring her back to Marseille, soak her in her tub, and keep her around for a few days.

On that score, Rose and those birds of passage understood one another very well. No sentimentality: fuck a little, not too adeptly, then love 'em and leave 'em, just like guys.

There were Homeric evening sessions there, with four or five sots finishing themselves off on red wine before getting into out-of-focus fighting with each other, during which they soiled the walls a bit more. I would hear them from my bedroom, for I always went up before their wine turned sour on them. Drunken women have always been a horror to me. Whenever I looked at Rose, ugly and neglected, I was reminded of a passage of Colette's:

> A woman who remains a woman is a complete being. She is lacking in nothing, especially when she is with her *amie*. But if she takes it into her head to try to be a man, she is grotesque. What could be sorrier or more ridiculous than a simulated man?

Rose was a living warrant of the widespread belief that all lesbians are ugly, that if they're lesbians, it's because no man would give them a tumble.

To make such a claim is to forget that some men are not very choosy and will shove their pricks into any gaping hole: dog, goat, Cholon duck, rubber water-skin filled with lukewarm liquid, to say nothing of a nice split prickly pear. No matter how ugly a woman, there will always be some man horny enough to have a go at her. To claim that we are lesbians because men didn't want us is once again to subordinate all our lives and our entire fates to the pleasure of the male alone, for he, no matter how ugly, will always have a chance to choose.

Why doesn't anyone say of a man that he turned gay because he was so unattractive no woman would have him? On the contrary, the handsomer he is, the more chance he will deviate, propositioned from schooldays on, sought after by other males like a choice bit of prey.

So a man has the option to select from among the most beautiful of beings, male or female. And ugly girls have no alternative but to resort to the well-known dildo!

That's too simple.

No, we don't wear ugliness as a uniform. When you come into my Katmandou club for the first time, you are amazed by the percentage of beautiful girls and gorgeous women who come there. A much higher percentage than in any straight joint. Our figures haven't been ruined by a series of pregnancies, our features not worn out by nights sitting up by cradles, or the toil of housework, doing laundry and washing dishes.

I must admit, alas! that not all lesbians take great pains to look attractive.

I have seen so many nicely made up, pretty, feminine-looking girls who, once they become lesbians, gradually move toward a very masculine kind of neuterness. They adopt the jeans-and-shirt uniform, use no makeup, have their hair done less often. That's what leads to the misunderstanding. Among ten such sloppily rigged-out kids, you'll find eight unaccented pretty faces, eight hidden pretty bodies. It isn't ugliness, it's plain lack of grooming.

While understanding such an attitude, I can't find it intelligent. It would seem to indicate that all the adornments, jewels, and bangles that women wear are nothing but gewgaws, deceptive fishing flies intended as bait for the male, for the seduction of their future children's progenitor, for bagging the pigeon from whom all good things flow. For women engaged in the tough struggle to find a nest, no weapon can be overlooked.

Among us, the competition is of another kind: a pouter pigeon décolleté or a pair of artificial lashes are not what will make a girl be the most loving and caressing of mistresses. We know how to judge a woman beneath her makeup and, looking at another who is the reflection of ourselves, how to read her unmasked face.

If some lesbians go on using makeup, dressing in the height

of fashion (created for us by gays), it is often only because their careers require it (fashion industry, show business, public relations) or because their lover insists that they show such femininity. Nevertheless, the gap between sloppy and sophisticated is wide enough for all of us to find our niches without any trouble. We love Woman, so we love her beauty. Why not, however discreetly, underline what nature has been good enough to give us?

Refinement, whether of dress or physical appearance, cannot but improve the individual.

Besides, the active straight woman has also relegated bras and rats and artificial tresses to the wardrobe bin. It is becoming hard to tell a lesbian businesswoman from a straight one. Newspaperwoman, lawyer, or boutique owner, all get their clothes from Ted Lapidus or Yves Saint-Laurent, and all have the same hairstyles from Maurice Franck or Jean-Louis David. The dried-up dyke, with colorless lips, dull tailored suit with man's necktie, a grotesque caricature of manhood, has had her day. On the other hand, if you come across a supersophisticated vamp these days, nine chances out of ten she's some drag queen who salvaged all the accessories and trinkets that we tossed away fifteen years ago.

Fake Marilyn Monroes don't draw anyone except at Madame Arthur's or the Carrousel.

In an issue of *Le Crapouillot* devoted to mannish women, there is a picture of a women's liberation demonstration in which the only feminine-looking blonde who has a triumphal display of cleavage is a former female impersonator from the Alcazar. However, those who want to show their girl friends an image of the stereotypical lesbian in body shirt and briefs can always find such fossils at the so-called femme cabarets that get by only by soaking the out-of-towners for the bubbly while letting them gawk at such shows.

These poor transvestites are often simple housewives who each night rent their tuxedoes from the cloakroom of your fantasies, gentlemen.

As for Rose, she got killed. Her car was crushed under a tanker truck. As she lay in the morgue, she had a calmer, more serene face than I had ever seen on her in life.

I tried to buy the property from her father, whom she had both hated and adored. He turned me down; he wanted the house to die, along with his daughter. Now it is just an old abandoned structure along the autoroute and when I go by it, I slow down and hang ten years of nostalgic, colorful memories from the torn-off shutters and the torn-up roof.

We went to Greece. As far as Lesbos. Lesbos, with its magic name. Poor little Greek island at the end of the world, with your cursed reputation; a veil of modesty has been cast over your name, and now they call you only by the name of your capital, Mytilene, because one Sappho, poetess by trade, who kept a school of kittens, not to say pussies, here, had the bad taste to jump off one of your high rocks—because of her love for one of her handsome male disciples (a fact that is too often overlooked).

There must have been a lot of geographical changes with time, because if Sappho were to jump from that rock today (with its memorial stele put up by American lesbians), she would probably do nothing but sprain her wrist. Too bad for a bisexual writer who left us her name for habits that she neither invented nor exclusively practiced.

I reject her as my standard bearer. I deny that this Sappho, the two-faced female Janus, has the right to be our patron saint.

However, let's not reject Sapphism only to fall into Elulaism, or "sisters in Lesbitude," as the poet might say. The only elders I recognize are still, alas, very close to us. In earlier centuries, true lesbians dared not show their faces; they would never have gotten by. They could at best only jollify their lives with a few women secretly loved. Our real forerunners are Renée Vivien, Natalie Clifford Barney, Radclyffe Hall, and Nicole Louvier, who has not been properly recognized.

But in Lesbos, with its name that delighted me, the hotels were amusingly named the Sappho, the Lesbion, and the like.

We did get accosted by one Lesbian, a male, a baker who was handsome as a god, but so what? Besides, between slim little Cat at twenty-three and me with my thirty-six-year-old bulges, I was the one he paid most attention to. Just my luck! He wouldn't let me out of his sight. Even if we sneaked out of the hotel hugging the walls, he was always there, kind, thoughtful, and unbearable. I got so sick of him that I actually did get sick.

I can't stand a man's interest in me. I had a real breakdown and we had to leave the island before we had planned. The irony of it was that virtually only in his arms could I drag myself to the boat, that's how sick I was.

The anchor barely weighed, and Lesbos with its Lesbians behind me, I suddenly miraculously recovered!

It was now two years since Cat had entered my life. We did not live together. She had kept her room at her parents' and slept there two or three times a week, for appearances' sake. I think they understood our relationship, but, like so many parents, preferred to act "as if."

We were happy; I was in love.

One day, I decided to go and spend a week in Paris, but Cat could not get away from her work. She accompanied me to the Marignane airport. This was not the first time we had been apart, far from it, especially since I had become a pollster, but for some unknown reason I was heartsick about it. As we waited for my plane, I asked her, "Do you want me to stay? I'm not all that anxious to leave you."

"No, no, go. You need the vacation."

In Paris, of course, I had dinner at the Casque. It was a delightful little restaurant on Rue Bonaparte, where gays and lesbians of the neighborhood got together among a clientele of tourists. Claude, the girl who (I think) still runs it now, used to work there with her parents. Her mother, a severe and rigid Alsatian type, ruled over the place. Naturally, she had no idea of her daughter's unorthodox life-style. The latter was a real lady-killer with overpowering blue eyes, and the mother was delighted with how well-behaved all her girl friends were.

"Just imagine," she would say, "no carryings-on, absolute decorum, the men dining on one side and the girls on the other."

And, indeed, by a sort of tacit agreement, the boys ate stage right and the ladies stage left.

The day she learned that Claude was a lesbian, she flipped out in private and in public. We girls no longer existed in her eyes. She didn't chase us away, but we just became invisible. Implore though we might, "Madame, please some bread; Madame, can we have a little water?" it remained the Sahel or the Gobi Desert to all intents and purposes. Claude alone looked after our needs.

So, as I said, the evening I got in I had dinner at the Casque, with a few sidekicks.

To them, I am "la Marseillaise," the gal from Marseille who from time to time comes to Paris to knock over the most appealing quail. They know me even if they've never seen me: Oriental type, long dark braid; since I seem to have enough to live on and a lot of time on my hands, and I live in Marseille, that great center of the drug trade, they've often supposed I had some ill-gotten gains, from narcotics, or the black market in piastres or dollars.

I let it slide off my back. After all, better to be considered dangerous than insignificant.

I'm introduced to a girl who seems likable, amusing, witty. Her name is Ghislaine de Something or Other. She goes for me, quite obviously. Big ass, heavy breasts, blond hair cut too short. She looks a little like Hardy Kruger, the movie actor, and is proud of it. That's her affair. Anyway, she amuses me, but doesn't interest me beyond that. I'm in love with Cat.

Ghislaine and I have dinner together the next night. She talks a lot, is brilliant and well-mannered, which is all to the good.

After this meeting, I get three telegrams and a bouquet of red roses from her a day. Her letters are wild, so lyrical as to be almost ridiculous, but her handwriting is very fine, high-class. She is wildly in love with me, begs me to let her sleep with me. Just sleep, nothing else.

Up in her little top-floor servant's room in the fancy 16th Arrondissement, she plays her guitar and sings songs to me that she composes quite well. I start softening. Okay, we'll sleep together. Just sleep, nothing more.

The night was long. Naked against each other, I could feel her hot, soft body, supple as foam rubber. First neck kisses, then cheek kisses, and after two hours we were kissing each other wildly, and an hour later I was letting her do me. At dawn, we had done it all. I had cheated on Cat, when I hadn't wanted to, when I was in love with her, and really didn't want any part of the big blond baby carrying on about me.

Ghislaine was thirty-nine, and still a virgin. Physically and morally untouched. A child. She was discovering love, orgasm, she was thrilled by it all, she said it so well and wrote me about it so fervently that when she came down to Marseille a week later to be with me, for all my resolutions I could not hold out, and I made love with her again.

That was the start of a stormy affair that was to last over a year. For the first time in my life, I was being unfaithful to the woman I loved.

Ghislaine was something else. Never, I believe, did I make love so much or with so much pleasure. Sure, I was a sensualist. I loved lovemaking. But with Ghislaine, the perfect partner, docile, ready for the most daring, the deepest of experiments, my imagination went wild. In hotel rooms we took the mirrored doors off the wardrobes to set them up so we could feed on our own image. I was thus able to keep forever the memory of her smooth, plump, pink, round rump, into which my nails dug cruel new furrows.

Once again, since I wasn't in love with her and therefore had no shame about me, no respect for her, I could give free rein to my every desire, my most exciting fantasies. Her thick white thighs were a temple into which I dived with frenzy, holding nothing back. I made her do everything, exacted it all of her, taught her everything, since she knew nothing and desired all of it and more.

Lesbians are accused of being infantile. Well, Ghislaine de Something or Other certainly was. Under the thumb of a widowed mother, a Scrooge in a skirt who had dubbed her sales manager of her dietetic products concern at a fancy salary, but actually paid her only the minimum guaranteed wage and pocketed the difference, Ghislaine once had tried to run away to Algeria with a girl friend. Her mother followed them there, caught them, put her leg over the balcony rail of their room, threatening to jump to her death below, and denounced the girl friend to the director of the hospital where she was a nurse.

Ghislaine, beaten and broken, went back home.

The more I got to know her, the more I felt she didn't really deserve any more than the minimum wage that her mother turned over to her. In the factory, she must have been worse than useless, probably more in the way of the rest of the staff than anything else.

So all her life she would remain a deficient child, deprived even of her heartbeats by that awful despot.

But that is not true of all lesbians. We are said not to have outgrown our childhood, to hang on to our schoolgirl crushes, to stagnate in dirty habits acquired in boarding or reform school. That we have never emerged from the transitional stage of adolescence, when sexuality has not yet reached full bloom. In a word, that we all remain arrested at fifteen—the age of Juliet, of violent, romantic passions. All right, we agree, that's what we are, so let us stay that way! Let's keep alive that bluebell of hope that no woman who's been through the trauma of her last child's case of measles will ever again have time to cultivate.

Yes, it's true, we are infantile to the degree that, for the most part, having no family to worry about, we remain open to the thousand delights of life.

Look at a married woman with children, a job, a house to take care of. At thirty-five, she looks her age. She looks like a lady, and fits right into the part.

If for one weekend she goes off with her lesbian sister or lesbian cousin and a group of the latter's friends, after a few hours a miracle will occur. She'll begin to relax, to feel happier, freer. She's shed ten years, become transfigured. Because, for that weekend, she has been released from the household worries, the harness of marriage, the family enslavements.

However, don't get the idea that our lives are just one long summer vacation. But when two women live together they share the household chores and on Sunday there won't be one of them glued to the football game on TV while the other does the week's ironing. Having children is not what ages women, but the chores of everyday life, on which her man grants her a monopoly. She's expected to be Mommy-the-Feeder until 10 P.M. and Messalina the minute the dish-washing apron comes off.

Whereas two lesbians share life more like two schoolgirls or sisters. And these little nothings are what make our lives easier and keep us younger.

The "grown-up" women who are held up to us as our opposites, the ones who can no longer afford to be "infantile" in their loves or their everyday behavior, often have to find solace in soap operas or advice-to-the-lovelorn columns.

Is that so much better?

That summer, Ghislaine, Cat, and I rented a villa at

Bandol. Cat adored Ghislaine and she returned the feeling. Her affection for Cat was sincere, without ulterior motives. We had finally come not to feel any guilt toward her because we both loved her so much, and since our relationship deprived her of nothing, I didn't think I had to fill her in on what we had going together.

Cat went into Marseille each morning to work, and came back to us at the end of the afternoon. We were alone together all day, and, as Geneviève put it, "the bells kept ringing for me and my gal."

Geneviève couldn't understand how I could go for that "fat cow," as she called her, anyway.

I couldn't either, to tell the truth. Her stupidity appalled me; her culture and wit, which had seduced me at first, had proved to be less than skin-deep. She was limited and erratic and, except for her fights with her mother and the fact that she looked like Hardy Kruger, could find nothing to talk about. I was constantly taking her to task in public, sometimes so rudely that Cat would call me on it. But the minute we were alone I plunged into the delights of her body.

She had a rose-colored cunt, delicately rose, with no aggressive brown or reddishness on the lips. Rose-colored as the flower of the same name, soft as cotton batting. My fingers, which had had first possession of her, were intimately acquainted with all the recesses within. In the eyes of the machos, and especially to gay males, we are nothing but "a hole." But no, we are not a hole; rather, a grotto. And go ask the speleologists whether any two grottoes are like. Each has its own separate character: rough edges, velvety, silken, or mossy texture, softness, hardness, moistness, deluge, lake, sea or rivulet, torrent or drought.

Our hands become as sensitive as those of safecrackers who rub their fingertips with sandpaper before touching forbidden doors, so that their touch becomes ultrasensitive. Thus, too, our fingers—they let us sense the slightest difference, know the hiddenmost folds of the insides of the other woman. We don't have a sonar with a scanning head to plunge into those depths, but an arm with a thousand soft, insinuating, vibrating tentacles each movement of which brings forth a sigh, a moan, an outcry.

Ghislaine had discovered fulfillment at my hands, and gave herself over to me bound hand and foot. She put up with all the reprimands because all she needed to do was close her eyes, even when I was insulting her, to feel me inside her, making her die with unknown pleasures.

As for me, despite my scorn for her, when I once again saw her nude, open, her milky body spread, offering itself, waiting to be taken, a panting slave, all I could think of was playing on that wonderful instrument of flesh, making every one of its strings vibrate more violently than ever before.

The way the mere sight of her aroused me brought me to her already in a sweat, opened out, thirsting for my own fulfillment.

Love with Ghislaine . . .

I remember a prairie between Toulouse and Bordeaux. Quick picnic between two clumps of greenery, and Ghislaine before whom I was on my knees, inhaling the aroma of her blond crotch, kissing it, while she was on edge, eye and ear on the qui vive, a fruit to be quickly devoured lest some voyeur come upon us, as she moaned her heart out, legs spread, arching back against the hood of her car.

If ever I was cunt-crazy, it was certainly with her. I loved her best only lying down, naked, my honey honey, slave to the flesh, moaning, screaming, inventive, magnificent mistress, marvelous lover.

What a wonderful coupling there is in the active mutuality of two women making love to each other. What an overwhelming thing to feel on one's lips a sex as moist as one's own, Ghislaine's, that rose cathedral between its two snowy pillars, crushing me under her full-blown downy body, fitting so snugly into my own, her heavy breasts rubbing against my belly, my groin, all of my skin, and her face burrowing into the very heart of my being. The same kiss, the same caress, the same rhythm, the same tempo, right up to the final bursting, the unleashing of the tempest.

Of course, we are narcissuses, gilded flowers looking at our own reflections in the pools and springs of our own eyes, our own cunts. We enfold ourselves in one another's arms and legs, roll ourselves up tightly in the fields of our sheets, enclosed in a universe to which the male is alien, a superfluous, bothersome, useless element, with no place in it.

Sometimes an idiot dyke, beating herself on the chest like Tarzan, will tell me, "I had a girl, not a lesbian. I was her first, and after me there were no more, she went back to straight fucking."

I answer, "What's that to brag about? You should have given her such a taste and love for woman that she could never again do without it. Your being the only one just means that you struck out! Big deal! Learn how to make love to a woman the way she ought to be made love to, and I can guarantee you that if she turns straight again, it'll only be for what she can get out of a man. You should have left her with such a longing for the shores she was coming off of thanks to you that all she would dream of after that would be slopes of cool downy growths, not steep bald peaks."

If I were a man, I'd be gay, for I am truly inverted. I can live and vibrate only in terms of my own sex. If I were a man, I would love the body and the sex of a man, my brother, my accomplice, my mirror.

In August, after Bandol, Cat and I were off to the Pyrenees. We were supposed to go up to Paris to see Ghislaine after that. I was happy to be alone again with my little Cat. We still got along just as well and I loved her as tenderly as ever.

A few days before we were to get to Paris, Ghislaine had a car accident; she broke her arm and was in the hospital. At her bedside, I finally met her mother.

In the course of a rain of insults, spat through tight lips pursed with hatred, she threatened to sue me, to send letters to my husband, my family, my employer, the press. She accused us of three-way orgies.

I laughed—it was so outlandish—but was kind of worried about all my own letters, which Ghislaine kept wrapped in a ribbon in her closet. If her mother were to find them, Cat would know all. Through the torrent of the old witch's recriminations, that was all that mattered to me. I wasn't listening to her.

She finally concluded, "I'd rather see my daughter dead than going on being a lesbian."

"Well, then you can stay and croak on top of your damned fortune, because your daughter is a lesbian and won't ever be anything else!"

So we turned second-story women. By way of the drainpipe and the eaves, Cat, turning cat burglar true to her nickname, slipped into Ghislaine's room. I found the letters, and carried them away. As we were crossing the Alma Bridge, I suddenly stopped the car and, before Cat knew what was happening, threw the only evidence of our affair into the Seine. Now she would never know.

For a month after that, it was all private-eye stuff and cheap melodramatics. Ghislaine's mother wanted to have her committed, on grounds of incompetence. She had a lot of money and not all doctors are above such considerations.

Joseph, the owner of the new lesbian spot, the Quod Libet, told me there was only one solution: Get her married. That way, her mother would lose her rights over her.

"If she wants, I'll marry her," he volunteered.

This was unhoped for—and very nice. Because to Joseph, Ghislaine was just another customer. But he was a young Egyptian Jew who was fairly mad in his own right.

We moved Ghislaine's stuff out during one night. The next morning, at the hospital, we came as a raiding party to pick her up, for fear her mother would put up a fight.

It was the Rape of the Sabines, the Abduction from the Seraglio—but mostly, the Pain in the Ass.

A fast wedding on a Saturday morning at the city hall in the 11th Arrondissement, mixed in among a score of other couples. Moiré gowns, Sunday best, clip-on bow ties, wedding cakes and white Jordan almonds. We weren't in keeping: Joseph, his young bride, Cat, and I, all in jeans, the bride with her arm in a cast and one of her eyes still boasting a shiner . . .

The next day we were off to Marseille, and now we had to find a job there for Ghislaine.

That was no easy matter. She didn't know how to do anything. She got up at noon to take a glance at the want ads. Nothing seemed worthy of her. She wasn't about to sell herself short.

I was now working for the French Institute of Public Opinion, in Marseille proper. I earned less, and it was harder, but I didn't have to travel so much. I was at home, between my two women. Ghislaine slept in the guest room on nights when Cat stayed over, since she still slept part of the time at her parents'.

Evenings when she wasn't there, as ever, it was passion, frenetic love, without the slightest remorse, and still I had such tender love for the one and such violent desire for the other.

Finally, a guy I knew suggested that I help him set up a little discothèque, upstairs in a restaurant in the Old Port.

If there is one infallible nighttime rule, it is that an upstairs spot never catches on. At night, the customers don't mind "going down" to a cellar, but they won't climb. They somehow prefer having to work their way up steps to get out in the wee hours. But I didn't know that golden rule yet, so I went ahead. This would give Ghislaine a chance to be a combination barmaid and deejay, and she'd earn her living.

The club was called Le Tacot [the Jalopy]. The décor

was minimal: a few posters of old cars and the usual upstairs restaurant furnishings, red imitation leather and formica. We installed some lighting and we were open for business.

There was room for about fifty people, but except for Sunday afternoons when we filled up with the younger set drinking soda-through-a-straw, we never had to turn anyone away.

I had given up my job polling now and acted as hostess and waitress to our very restricted clientele. Cat, when she finished her lab work, would come and run the turntable till we closed at two in the morning. We made out, by hook or by crook. It seems I was good as a hostess. The owner of Le Tacot had a big dance palace on the beach at the end of the Prado. He asked me to come and manage it. I turned him down.

I was quite amenable to running a club, as I was doing, for a while, and for fun, but not to make a career of it. Then he offered to make me manager of a restaurant-lounge on the Old Port. I hesitated a little. The terms were attractive, the work not distasteful, I felt I could do it, especially with Cat to help out, but the hours that restaurant work entailed, 8 A.M. to 2 A.M., turned me off. And besides, there was no way to take a few days off now and then. It was like penal servitude. My natural indolence and deep taste for independence flared up. I turned that down too.

Ghislaine, originally slated to break in as a barmaid, broke glasses and undercharged. She had become an additional ball and chain. Too heavy to carry. Neither Cat nor I could go on supporting her forever. Being good at lovemaking is great, but it isn't everything.

I finally had to make her understand that she'd do just as well to run back to Mommy's skirts. She was beyond salvation. Her mother had ruined her for life. She had turned her into a big rag doll, unable to shoulder any responsibilities, raised to marry a comfortable bourgeois and turn out babies in a big town house. But a grain of sand had somehow gotten into the works: The broodmare was lesbian and would never lay a man, not even to "make ends meet," as so many others would.

Beyond that, sweet, tender, harmless, disarming, childish Ghislaine has become embittered. She realized her life was one big failure. Since there wasn't a mean bone in her body, she couldn't even hold it against her mother. She just saw she was a cipher. Three years before, she had tried suicide, as a way out. She had muffed even that. With the scars on her wrists, she had slunk back to Paris, and her mother had been magnanimous about it, giving her back her job, her title—and her minimum wage.

While she now had to come back once more with her tail between her legs, she did hold out on one point, the only one, in fact, on which she had ever stood up to the old lady: not to live at home with her mother. That was her only survival, her only consolation: to be able freely to love the women she wanted.

She moved in "temporarily" with her nominal husband Joseph, and stayed on over a year. When he finally asked her to move out, she threatened to sue him for divorce, alleging adultery and demanding alimony. That would have been easy: Joseph, one of the greatest cocksmen the world had ever known, every morning came home with one or even two dames that he had gone and picked up in some other joint after the Quod Libet closed.

He shrugged. Being a fatalist and a nonviolent Oriental, he simply laughed away the whole thing.

Ghislaine finally took off on her own.

She dropped out of our sight. After a number of affairs, some successful, some not, she accepted the fate of the no-longer-young bourgeoisified lesbians who don't go out to nightclubs any more but get together of a Saturday evening over a game of gin rummy and lime-blossom-and-mint tea.

Meantime, Joseph had fallen in love and really wanted to

get married. So Ghislaine agreed to a divorce, provided he took care of all the expenses. End of Ghislaine.

But that did not come till later.

Once Ghislaine had gone back to Paris, Cat and I were alone together again. Physical desire had died between us through my fault, because I can't be making love to two women at the same time, as I respect each one too much. And Ghislaine had completely absorbed me for months. So, Cat had gone to fairly freeish ways. Unobtrusively, tacitly, tenderly. She had her own little love affairs in Marseille and I, when I went to Paris, went back to my one-night stands: Natasha, beautiful and secretive, Virginia, full of pulp and juicy, Sylvia, obstinate, fascinating, and stupid.

CHAPTER VI

THERE WERE NO LESBIAN CLUBS ON THE RIVIERA. AT Cannes, in the old days, we used to go to the Jungle, Casanova, or the Trois Cloches, gay bars, but in the past two years some of them had shut down and the others had no room for us in the summer season. Dykes were all right in the slack season, but as soon as every gay guy of France and Germany descended on Cannes, they slammed the doors in our faces.

The previous summer, during our stay at Bandol with Ghislaine, about ten of us had arranged to meet at the Festival on the Croisette in Cannes. They came from Cassis, Saint-Tropez, Monte Carlo, or like us from Bandol. We were going to make a great evening of it. At two in the morning we were still roaming the streets, turned away from some of the clubs, frowned on at others, forbidden to dance together in most. All that was left us was the hookers' dives and the sailors' joints.

We split up, disappointed, after a final cup of coffee on the terrace of the Festival, and a last shot from me: "Next year there'll be a lesbian club in Cannes, even if I have to start it myself!"

That offhand challenge began to take shape in my mind. That was just the way we had gone about starting the Petite

Auberge, and somewhat the way I had become a schoolteacher. "Why not?" I ask myself, as I look at the water—and in I plunge.

I had some slight discothèque experience at Le Tacot, I knew all the gay girls on the Coast since I'd been coming to Cannes and Saint-Tropez for fifteen years, so they would be my basic clientele. Joseph would send us Parisian lesbians on vacation. I looked for a spot, and had a lot of luck. I was told about a woman who owned a big cabaret with a small discothèque attached to it. I went to see this sumptuous lady, a cathedral with embers for eyes, and laid out my plan with all the foolhardiness of the naive.

References? I hadn't any. But then, there were no lesbian clubs on the Côte d'Azur despite the wide potential clientele. Could I use her little discothèque for the summer? She was agreeable.

Ever ready to employ amateurs, I took as my barmaid one of Cat's lovers, and as deejay a nurse from Marseille—for the first few months. Later, we'd see. I had enough friends who could take over if needed.

Corinne, the landlady, supplied a cashier who would keep the accounts (I was in on a percentage deal, so it was normal for her to want to keep an eye on the take) and could act as an extra barmaid if the going got too heavy.

I opened up on June 28, 1967. I had sent out no more than a dozen invitations. Over a hundred people showed up on the first night!

My "Quod Libet Azur," as I had named it with Joseph's blessing, was a small but refined and well-appointed room, in polished wood, with a big log fireplace and a tiny dance floor alongside a horseshoe bar.

Every lesbian from Nice, Cannes, Haut-de-Cagnes, and as far away as Saint-Tropez was there. It had been years since we'd had a club we could call our own—since the time of the Klou, run by a woman called Léo, who was so stereotypical that everyone addressed her as "Sir."

Not since the old days when, on vacation at Saint-Tropez, we came for an evening and had to drive back at dawn over the Estérel ridge, so hard to negotiate at four in the morning. Now there was the autoroute, and the Tropezians could come and go at will.

I was the one who opened the door and did the serving. I was inflexible with men. They were allowed in only if accompanied by known girl friends who guaranteed their behavior. As for the male homosexuals, I paid them off in kind: "You weren't having any of us last summer? Well, now go dance on your own!"

At any rate, I have never been too happy in the company of gay males, especially the limp-wrist nances, those sad clowns who will always gladly bare their ass if they can just be queen for the evening. It is true, they provide inexpensive entertainment and are therefore often popular as dinner guests. We, on the other hand, are generally found dull and not entertaining. Women, whether lesbian or not, were not on the long end of the stick when senses of humor were being parceled out. Few of us abound in it. Besides, we're less exhibitionistic, much more modest, than the "get her!" crazies.

We, being women, are by our very nature less exuberant, more discreet. Men are the ones who hold noisy banquets and wild stag dinners. I think that of all the court jesters in French history only one was a woman, at the court of Henri IV when he was still King of Navarre.

If I have few gay male friends, my real pals are straight men, not women. Horizontally, I'll take the latter, but in an upright position I prefer people like Boris Vian, Pierre Kast, Caude Berri, Boris Bergman, or Roger Vailland, for instance —to mention only those whose names you may know. And if they become my friends, it's because they're not phallocrats, not so macho that their virility comes marching in before them. I don't look on them as males, that is, as the opposite sex, the opposite shore, the Martian, the unknown, but rather as brilliant companions who enrich my life and keep it amusing.

Quod Libet Azur, then, was a success. Corinne, my "landlady," left me full latitude to screen my clientele and run the club as I saw fit.

Unfortunately, she met up with a horrible dyke, a six-footer with lacquered wavy hair and diamond stickpin, and a chauffeured Rolls-Royce waiting outside the club all evening. This "lady" laid siege to Corinne all summer with so much tenacity and Dom Pérignon that finally she brought her around. She dragged our majestic-looking owner through such emotional brouhahas that Corinne's husband, who had been closing his eyes to it all up to then, finally divorced her.

Now Corinne owns an American bar in Paris. When we meet, we talk of old times in Cannes and smile about it all.

For my part, after one last erotic session with Ghislaine, who had come down from Paris for the Quod Libet Azur opening, I was at liberty and looking for a summer lover.

The one I selected was a rather ordinary girl from Nice, but a demon in bed. Sometimes, when we closed up, we went to Nice to sleep at her place. The sunrise on the beach washed away the smokiness of the night. We would devour some liver pâté on slices of bread, make love, and fall asleep around noon. With that kind of schedule, I didn't have much beach time. I hated civilized, dressed-up, sophisticated beaches with parking meters alongside that you have to have change for before you can leave your car and go bathing. Where was my immense beach at Pampelonne, with its bamboo cabanas in which we used to hole up without any clothes, with our fresh tomatoes, cold chicken, and the nice little rosé wine bought at a nearby farm?

In August, Cat was on vacation and came to tend bar while Joseph, who had closed his Paris spot for the summer, spent his nights in our club, handling the discs and creating a wonderful ambience. It was all fun and games, and in two months I earned more than in a semester of teaching or half a year of poll-taking.

A few days before we were to close up, at the end of August, a petite Parisienne came up to the bar, asking, "What do I owe?"

"Nothing," I replied, fascinated by the line of her lips, reminiscent of a Khmer Buddha, and her green-and-gold eyes. I said as much. It was the start of a new affair. Christiane was shy, antisocial, unpredictable.

She was some kind of secretary, with one hell of a face and a figure that was a bit heavy but well proportioned. She left Cannes without our having exchanged more than a few fervent kisses.

I closed up, spent a few days in Italy with my friend from Nice so as to kiss her off without heartache, and rushed up to Paris to join Christiane.

She lived over in Ménilmontant in a tenth-floor-walkup maid's room. I really had to want her badly to wear myself out climbing those lousy stairs, use the seatless Turkish crappers at the end of the hallway, and mark time in the traffic jams on the outlying boulevards. I was living on the other side of Paris at Joseph's, on Rue Boileau, from which Ghislaine, still his wife, had not yet moved out, and Christiane refused to sleep in such crowded quarters. So I had to climb those ten flights or forget it. Ten flights it was!

She had a compact, animal, hot, delicious body. The Japanese soldiers during the war had had a musky sugary smell I had adored. Now I had only to close my eyes, nostrils aquiver, to have her body greet me deliciously with the same aroma, a souvenir from the heart of Asia.

What did I do in Paris? Not much, to tell the truth. I was living on what I had made during the summer and from time to time worked a bit for Joseph, who was launching a new club, the Bacchus, in the Marais quarter. I handled the drinks when the barmaid was sick for a few weeks, stood in for Joseph when he wanted to take advantage of my presence to have a short vacation or go chasing skirts in other clubs. He had seen me at work during the summer and was quite willing to leave the management to me.

The Bacchus was going over like a house on fire. It was a beautiful vaulted cellar decorated with naked slabs of stone and animal skins thrown over deep couches.

There were lots of men. Many too many already. But Joseph, being a man himself, was hardly able to judge how crowded it was and how disagreeable they made it. It was here that I became conscious of what we represented to society, and what men thought and knew about us. Up to that time, I had known the company only of those I had been willing to put up with, and of the rest I had encountered nothing but the lovely cracks they're so good at tossing at you on the street: "You're just the right size for me, babe," "Going my way, chickie?" "Sweet one, how about a little fuck?" and other such greasy endearments.

But here now I was confronted with the mass of males, who, not having been rigorously screened out at the door, came in as conquerors, dressed to the nines and on parade, self-assured, certain that sooner or later, inevitably, the quail would fall out of the sky and right into their laps. What imbecilic theories, wild judgments, heartbreakingly stupid assertions, and deficient reasonings I had to listen to!

Men are either ill informed, in which case they should keep still and just watch and listen, or else they have completely misunderstood. Those are beyond hope. Just a very few have ever really tried to understand, to be openminded about it, neither aggressive nor paternalistic. They are the white blackbirds, and blessed be they!

Men who frequent lesbian joints fall into three categories: group-sex freaks, "problem types," and the ones who couldn't care less.

The last named are the nicest. They come to our clubs

because they know they won't be hustled by hookers and if they get into a conversation with a woman they won't feel obliged to make a pass so as not to offend her. They look on us as chums, and we're better to look at than chums in street suits. They sit at the bar, pay no attention to what's going on on the dance floor, drink, make conversation, relax, pay, and go their way. When I refer to them, I say, "Those aren't men. They're friends."

The "problem types," the guilt-ridden, the impotent, the superpotent, masochists, shy, overly self-confident—in a word, those who are having a hard time handling their complexes—come among us lesbians looking for reassurance. They say we make love better than straight women because we are more active and more enterprising. Obviously! How would a straight woman ever have learned how in the limited field of the coital bed, where the male, as a rule, makes the rules even though he himself most often is self-taught? Who taught him to kiss, to caress, to make love?

A few porno books read between the sheets at boarding school, or a few trips to whorehouses while he was in the service? How many of them were lucky enough to be initiated by an older woman, especially one sufficiently liberated so she taught them what to do and what not to do, and what a woman really likes? Poor things, they have to depend on their intuition alone, their own inspiration, and not all of them have the gift.

So those are amazed to find in us women who move, take the initiative, make suggestions. That is, when I say "us," I am going a bit afield since I don't really consider such women true lesbians but rather amiable Jills-of-all-trade. And besides, these neurotic men think their conquest is the greater for having been less easy, when they make it with girls who, presumably, don't usually go for the male gender. That is true. They do make it, but most of the time theirs are not such glorious conquests, not such great victories. They're jackals, devouring the carrion in a moment of unguardedness, such as the time I went back to Guy the night I discovered Gisou was nothing but a cheap harlot. They storm bastions that have just been waiting for a chance to make a temporary surrender.

Also, at times, they are merely the live dildo for a girl who is bored or has been alone too long. They make do with these scraps of love, leftovers of passion, illusory banners of their ludicrous conquests. They gloat, they're reassured, they crow over it. For all the good it does them!

Finally, there are the group-sex freaks, the ones who go in for what used to be called daisy chains.

Ah! To watch two women making love to each other! That's a wonder. They would be disgusted at the ugliness of sexual relations between faggots, but they drool with envy and a "purely artistic" delight at two lesbians entwined.

They try to become their good pal, their nice ambiguous friend just waiting for the moment when they can unexpectedly slip in between the two and plant their little emblem of endurance. How many women have thus been initiated into lesbianism "thanks" to their husbands or their lovers!

It is they who push, persuade, sometimes even force them into these three-way hookups. The women are too shy, too modest to accept such arrangements offhand. They might like to try with another woman, but that would be alone, not in the presence of their husband or lover. But to let him watch! . . . Finally, they give in, subject themselves to it, are surprised, begin to like it, and then go wild for it. One day, they discover there's one too many in the room and the bed, and the gent finds himself kicked out of the bed, driven from the room—even from her life. He swears, too late, that he'll never try that tack again!

How many such turned-out lovers, disestablished husbands I have met, who, because of this, detest us, refer to us as dirty dykes, and forbid their next female to set foot in our dens of iniquity!

Well, thanks be to them: they are our best suppliers!

I have never come across any true *ménages à trois.* There may be some, made up of a man and two nonlesbian women, in which he is the center of a circle at which two totally independent radii meet without ever touching.

When there are two lesbians and a man, it's not the same chemistry. There is no catalysis. We are too exclusive to tolerate a foreign element within our couple, whether male or female.

Oh, yes, I was forgetting one other category of men: those who cordially hate us. These, holding us responsible for their own fears, abhor us in their worry that they won't be able to satisfy us. Forget them . . .

My girl from Nice had come on again a month after I left Cannes. She had returned to the Bacchus and slit her wrists a little with a hunk of broken glass, at the top of the stone steps. She might easily have hurt herself very badly, doing her imitation of Jean Marais in the last act of *The Eagle Has Two Heads.* Fortunately, a compassionate arm caught her on the second step. All she had to show for it was a couple of pieces of adhesive tape, and I was good and angry.

I can't stand people who put on acts, especially those who try to blackmail you through suicide. This is the last resort of the weak, and therefore unfortunately that of abandoned women. I couldn't see that that added to my glory in any way, the way some lady-killers boast about how many suicides adorn their boutonniere.

Most of the time, suicides are failed fake suicides—that is, when the friend who was expected to come in as a lifesaver didn't arrive at the prescribed moment. That's why it's best to do what the really artful blackmailers do: call someone on the phone *before* taking the fatal step. It's safer that way.

I was with Christiane, to be sure, but I still had some rather wild side trips. For instance, that stripper from the Crazy Horse with her superb leather boots and straps who carried me away so cavalierly one fantastic night, or the constipated little snob who raped me in the toilet of the Saint-Hilaire, but they didn't mean anything. They were just the usual reaction of my bored body at those times when my heart was up for grabs.

The Bacchus had become the "in" place for night people. Since late suppers were served on the upper floor, there were days when we didn't finish until ten or eleven o'clock in the morning.

The staff of Carroll's, Elle et Lui, the whores from the Rue Saint-Denis, the questionable and distasteful nightbugs crawling out from under the rocks, came together here without too many conflicts.

Joseph navigated through it all beamingly and rarely had to turn in without company. There was fucking up, down, and around that whole place of his on Rue Boileau! Sighs, laughter, practical jokes—like the time he asked me to break into the bedroom and throw a jealous scene as if I were his wife, so he could get rid of a girl he wasn't able to shake.

Fat Ghislaine was still in the picture, with her latest girl friend, a French teacher. They slept in Joseph's bed and grumbled at having to get up and let him take possession of the warm sheets, when he got home at 8 A.M.—on such rare occasions as he did get there that early.

My winter in Paris went off in wild disorder, but I was having fun, discovering a world and a milieu I had until then known nothing about.

Unfortunately, the Cannes spot burned down during the winter. So, if I was to work that summer, I'd have to find another location.

"Why not in Saint-Tropez?" asked Picolette, an old acquaintance from the Trois Fontaines. She and Lila Brasseur owned one of the best restaurants in Saint-Tropez.

She thought I ought to go and talk to the Gorilla, the hairy café owner who had served breakfasts to every real celebrity in the world. He had a nice little club, just beyond the port, called the Yeti.

We made an arrangement to open at Easter, with Joseph and me alternating, trading places with each other at the Bacchus in Paris and the Yeti in Saint-Tropez.

Up to that time, the Yeti had had various kinds of seasons: from so-so to lousy.

I opened it in April 1968. My girl pals from Nice and Cannes dropped in. In Saint-Tropez itself, there were three famous lesbians who called all the shots: They took a liking to me and brought all their friends.

Men were as strictly prescreened as ever. Again I opened the door and did the serving; there was Christiane, my Parisian girl friend, whom I had dragged with me, as deejay, and a Vietnamese girl who had an antique shop in the Vaucluse Department came in to tend bar. As usual, all amateurs!

Easter was gray, rainy, as it so often is on the Riviera. April went by quietly. Cat came from Marseille for weekends, ever faithful, ever present, ever dear to my heart.

One tires of everything, but much more quickly of the strange and the disconcerting. That was the kind my Christiane was. It was her character more than her tenth-floor walkup that had worn me out. After Easter, I shipped her back to Joseph at the Bacchus, by special handling, and in return got his Paris deejay and barmaid, two pretty blond, very feminine girls, wild about each other. It was a delight to the eyes, an esthetic experience, to see them kiss, their hair merging, two fields of gold, pink lips, and aquamarine eyes.

I remained at the door, a pitiless sentry, turning away celebrities and members of the Cabinet alike if they were not already acquaintances of mine, but welcoming the cook from the Escale, who was a friend. This was almost one of the basic reasons we were a hit. Everyone wanted in to the little lesbian joint that was the "real thing" and so hard to crash.

That was when the May 1968 student explosion took place. But how can anyone talk about May 1968 who only experienced it at Saint-Tropez? Our only demonstration took place along the wharf between two *pastis,* from L'Escale to Sénéquier's, one morning when it was not nice enough to go fishing or play *pétanque.* The rest of the time, we listened to the news on a transistor while sunning nude in one of the deserted coves, and over the radio we heard the explosion of the tear-gas canisters as we sat on a café terrace before a highball. Our only rationing was ten francs' worth of gas per car per day, and for a while there were no more filter-tip Gitanes to be had, but then, I didn't even smoke . . .

Once the last barricade was gone, Parisians poured onto the autoroute to the South, descended on us in flocks, relieved, anxious for relaxation and letting go. The Yeti was crammed solid. I met a lot of celebrities who were new to me, and I was as excited as a kid who finally sees a star "in person."

I had known some of the most famous, like Marcel Camus, Boris Vian, and Roger Vailland, but I hadn't had occasion to meet many actors, comedians, singers, painters, or millionaires.

One famous American movie mogul, past his prime, came in with his latest conquest, a French model, whom he was of course going to put into pictures. His fantasy was to see two girls make a play for each other. His girl would ask another to dance, and none ever refused, for she was gorgeous. The champagne flowed like water at their table, and then the two gals would disappear. He imagined them in the john finishing each other. In fact, they were just out having a smoke.

When they came back, the producer was delighted, but skillfully concealed the fact behind his big cigar and dark glasses, and then he would slip a thousand francs to the pickup, whom his girl had in the meantime clued in.

When she and the pickup *really* went for each other, they would meet secretly, during the day, at the Byblos. That was a common site for such assignations—once, it was reported, a chambermaid there had opened a door and surprised a great lady of France and a delightful chanteuse who had literally gone "into the closet" on hearing her approach . . .

Since news travels fast, I was also renewing acquaintance with old friends I'd lost touch with. A Marseille hairdresser, handsome as a Greek shepherd, who had been in a car accident and dragged from hospital to hospital for a year, stuffed with morphine, before his leg was amputated. He hobbled around on his artificial limb, handsome as ever, but bitter, finished. He could still afford a gigolo but had no taste for it. Addicted through all the morphine the medics had pumped into him, he clipclopped around for another summer and then ended it all with an overdose.

There was Yves C., also hopelessly lame, whom I had so hated when he and I shared Geneviève's favors. He still had gorgeous creatures in tow and still misused them just as badly. What was the crippled devil's charm? He was now a famous painter living in the U.S. We had ignored each other for twenty years, meeting perhaps a dozen times at cocktail parties in Paris or Megève, and all of these times politely "not identifying." But now that I was running a club I couldn't let personal grudges interfere with business unless they were really serious. So, when Yves C. said, "Bury the hatchet?" I laughed and shook hands.

I am not used to celibacy, and am not compatible with it. Sleeping in an empty bed is intolerable to me. I'd rather feel a body and feminine warmth, even if I'm not in love. It is wonderful to turn over in one's sleep and find one's hand on a soft skin, a shapely curve, something warm . . .

I set my sights on a big blond thing, a real tomboy with a big nose, missing teeth, but splendid green eyes and long gorgeous legs. Her name was Michèle, and she ran the turntable at the Pigeonnier, a gay bar.

When she came to the Yeti, after the Pigeonnier's closing hour, I asked her to lead me in a dance. She enveloped me in her immense arms and I felt protected. This was a new feeling for a habitual conqueror. The Yeti closed. It was seven in the morning, and the crews of the yachts in the port were beginning to swab down the decks. We kissed on the wharf-side. I have never liked to shock people, or make a show of myself. But Michèle looked so much like a boy with her tousled short hair that we were easily taken for a conventional pair of lovers! My friends were taken aback by this new crush of mine. She was so unlike my usual type. But she was intelligent, cultured, witty, funny, wild, secretive, and passionate.

Pretty soon, the most famous gay males, attracted by the fact that Tout-Saint-Tropez flocked to the Yeti, came on in to join the show-biz celebs and great lesbians and chanteuses who were already habitués.

In my three years at the Yeti, Brigitte Bardot was about the only one who never dropped in. Was she afraid it might compromise her reputation? I doubt that. In Saint-Tropez, people's doings and morals are neither a problem nor an object of curiosity. It is doubtless one of the great capitals of tolerance and discretion, and had she been a lesbian even the scandalmongering papers would not have heard about it.

In mid-July, as planned, we were to switch spots, but the Bacchus had folded. There had been too many men, and the usual thing had happened: the girls had started to leave, and the men followed after them. The Bacchus's landlady had another ailing disco, near the Opéra, called the Microthèque. Joseph had taken that over now, and planned to give it a new start, as a lesbian joint, of course.

So Joseph came down to spell me. I was a bit afraid of this switch, for my clientele was quite different from the Bacchus's. Would he and they get along with each other?

I was no ordinary hostess; I greeted my friends, introduced them to one another, every evening trying to create a room as harmonious as a well-arranged bouquet, putting one here, another there. With Joseph, it was all camaraderie, jokes, a slightly ambiguous atmosphere, and high decibels.

I was in for quite a surprise in Paris: at the end of July, the

Microthèque was closing down for a month. Joseph knew it, but had not even mentioned it to me, fearing that I might back out. That would leave me high and dry for half the summer. It hadn't been very nice of him. The Riviera was my turf, Paris his, and our switch was meant as what in the Midi was called "a good turn," nothing more. I was furious at him.

The landlady watched me at work for a week, and then suggested that I take over the disco without Joseph when it reopened. Naturally, I started by refusing, but she patiently came back to it. Under no circumstances was she taking Joseph back. It was me or nothing. At the same time, alarming rumors came up from Saint-Tropez. My old clientele was evaporating, replaced by a very different one of Joseph's, and the Gorilla wrote me that next year I would have to remain in charge all summer.

I remembered that the biggest Parisian lesbians had said to me, "Come on to Paris. There's no good spot there. It's just waiting for you."

I answered that I'd never undertake anything in Paris so long as Joseph was there, because it was his territory.

I was still undecided. On the one hand, there was the memory of how he had bailed out fat Ghislaine, offered his hospitality for a whole winter, and been disarmingly nice. On the other, my business arrangements with him had flopped, he had played me a really lousy trick, and adventure was beckoning.

I still hesitated for a bit, he and I exchanged some bittersweet letters, and finally I agreed to take over the Microthèque. I felt I was losing a brother.

From now till September, there was nothing to keep me in deserted Paris, and I went back down to the Riviera. That was my home. From Marseille to Monte Carlo, so many memories, so many women strewn along my path. I remembered, going through Juan-les-Pins, now the kingdom of crêperies and pizza parlors, my first summer in France, in 1947, that August at my uncle the papermaker's, the villa next door to Mistinguett's who used to invite us in for a drink (in those days, it was still referred to as an apéritif), the beaches of La Garoupe and Eden Roc, where the poor little repatriated student, ugly and despondent because of the flatness of her chest, tried to blend into the scenery.

Now, I was going to go back to Paris. Oh, just for a year or two, I didn't think that running a discothèque could keep me interested any longer than that . . .

Thus, in September 1968, the start of my Parisian nights.

I rented an apartment large enough so I could share it with Michèle, my friend, who would run the turntable, and Cat, who, having quit her laboratory job, would tend bar, as well as Dominique, who had come up to spend a period of detached service at the Ministry of Finances and decided to stay on with me.

We were a houseful. My solar system, stars and planets, revolved around me. I acted as waitress, after greeting the customers and seeing them to their tables; the landlady ran the cash register, and upstairs a doorgirl checked coats.

Soon, we were overwhelmed and I had to hire a girl to help me wait tables. Then I was able to give myself more fully to what had become my only job: greeting and making conversation, table-hopping, with a nice comment for everyone, seeing to it that ice and drinks were replenished, smoothing over the rough spots, helping people have a good time, smiling always and forever, being jolly, funny if I could; in a word, being "on" all the time.

Every night, I talk, listen, give answers.

Every night, I get asked the same questions, for, every night, there is at least one beginner or novice, brought in for the first time by her girl friends. Their questions are always the same, and I often wished I had a cassette along, with the answers prerecorded.

The most bothersome part is that an intelligent man who wants to understand asks the same questions as the idiot who wants to make wisecracks or convert us. Women are always curious, never hostile, often upset by what they are discovering. If their questions are the same, it is because man has taught them the same prejudices, the same preconceived ideas.

And I am the Doña Quixote knocking over all those windmills.

But male hostility is always there, waiting, ready to break out, hiding behind irony or feigned condescension.

How to convince them that we are not all "disappointed" women? Disappointed by them, it goes without saying, because they absolutely have to have a part to play in it—even if it's only that of the bad guys.

Very few lesbians are virgins. Often, they've been married, have had children, and are not sorry about it. Some try from three to seven male experiences, spaced over a period of ten years or so. At times, some dark horse will succeed in retaining their interest for a few weeks or months, but they inevitably come back to their deeper truth.

Naturally, virgin lesbians are challenged with, "How can you know you don't like something, if you've never tried it?"

To which I answer, "Not everybody has a yen to eat shit."

One can feel such revulsion for the male that she has no desire whatever to give him a try. That is true for about five percent of lesbians who are otherwise physiologically and psychically completely normal. But watch out! I said *revulsion*, not fear of the male, as he prefers to fancy it.

Of course, if you've already slept with men, the "seducer" will allege that you didn't "get a fair shake" from the ones who preceded him. By trying harder, persevering, surely you will—so, why not let him be the one?

But why should we look for the rare blackbird who'll make us swoon with that little something extra he has, when we are perfectly satisfied in the arms of women, any and all women, brunettes, blondes, dogs, beauties, cats, or tigresses?

Life is too short, lovetime too short, to waste one's efforts in seeking out a pleasure one gets along so well without.

Why should I have to overcome my lack of desire for the masculine body, the texture of its skin, its odor, its breath, its sex, its hair, when I bathe in the bodies of my sisters, eyes wide open, nostrils palpitating, hands devouring?

No, let's not waste the time; no, let's not waste the women we might love and hate, caress and leave.

Cat had lots of affairs. Almost any old kind, to tell the truth, and I was rather unhappy for her sake. She deserved better than these flashy birds on the wing. I gave her all of my tenderness, but that was not enough.

She gave me a monkey for a birthday present, a poisoned gift if there ever was one.

At first I was beside myself with joy, for I adored monkeys. I had had one in Indochina when I was seven, and still talked longingly about it. But I'd never have dreamed of keeping one in a Paris apartment.

The poor thing had to live in the kitchen, at the end of a long rope. The minute you came into the apartment, a wild-animal odor assailed you. "Smells like the circus," Geneviève would say when she called on me.

Michèle was wild about Olive (the monkey's name). She made him fringed suede jackets to match her own, and knitted him sweaters.

Since she now had a steady job at my place, she was able to have her nose done, her teeth replaced; her hair had grown longer and she had become very beautiful.

That was when I started getting a little tired of her, as if the butterfly that came out of the cocoon had lost interest for me.

Josette started coming on to me. She was a tall brunette, rather beautiful, with a great deal of charm but mainly a ridiculous nasal twang. We had met in Cannes the summer before, and she had become a pal who was fun.

Her sudden serious interest took me by surprise. I don't usually care for such switches in manner and she was decidedly lacking in mystery. But she stated her love for me with such sincere, soft faithful dog's eyes that I was touched. I let her talk me into it. We saw each other two or three times secretly. After that, since I don't know how to pretend and I imagined Michèle was only moderately attached to me, I said to her without preamble one evening in a taxi on the way to the Microthèque, "You know, we'll have to split up. I'm with Josette now."

She sighed and began to tremble, from head to foot, without uttering a word. When we got to the club, she went right on trembling in my arms, still without a reproach or a tear. It got worse: a quivering eagle, shot down in full flight. She, the proud one, the cold one, was croaking, but with dignity. I was dumbfounded, I had not wanted to hurt her like this. If I had imparted our split-up to her so baldly, it was only because I honestly thought it would roll right off her.

She went on loving me for a long time. It took her years to get over it. When, from time to time, I bump into her, she takes me tenderly in her arms, which are still as long as ever—neither of us has left the other with a bad or distasteful memory.

Josette did not last long. She talked a lot, thought herself irresistible, but while she "took off" well, her follow-through was disappointing. She was neither Don Juan nor Casanova—just a pretty nonentity who spent more time bragging than doing. She leaves so slight an impression that those who knew her hardly remember her. In our short time together, I was often unfaithful to her.

Next there was a delicious little Belgian girl, beautiful and stupid, of course, who was never to succeed in having a normal orgasm because she and her young husband, a bit of a stylist and more than a little gay, had gotten into such "bad habits," masturbating alongside one another without any other form of intercourse.

She knew nothing of passionate embraces; she did not like stroking her partner, and having another caress her gave her less satisfaction than when she did it herself.

Yet she screwed a lot of men, and women, too; she was beautiful and just a girl who couldn't say no. She pretended to be having an orgasm in order to make them happy, and her partners were never any the wiser.

But how can a woman pretend before another woman without being seen through? We are not blind, nor that credulous. So she quietly confessed all that to me, when I questioned her after my second or third failure to make her happy.

"Well, then, do yourself," I told her.

Stretched out alongside her, leaning on my elbow, I watched her, admiring her long hand, her red nails, like drops of blood between her wide-open thighs.

It was beautiful, it turned me on. My God, how beautiful she was!

"I just can't," she finally murmured. "I think that I can only do it in front of my husband; I'm used to it. You bother me, you turn me off . . ."

She was even selective about her voyeur! I regretfully had to let her return to their connubial masturbatory duets.

Just when needed, her exact opposite turned up. A long elusive liana, with almond-shaped green eyes and a cello of a voice. She had hardly sat down when I asked her to dance. As that evening I had had one of what I call the occupational hazards of my job—that is, I had drunk a bit more than I should—I came on to her very quickly. The creature was all for it. We kissed languorously, during a whole set of slow dance numbers.

I saw her back to her table and returned to the bar. One of the women habituées said to me, "You know who that is you're making a play for?"

"Why, yes," I said, "one beautiful creature."

"No," she replied, "he's a transvestite."

My heart flipflopped. I went back to the airy blonde, and said, "I'm sorry about what just happened, but I thought you were a woman."

"No harm done. On the contrary. I loved dancing with you. Can't we do it again?"

"Sorry. But I don't go for men, and you're one of them."

"Oh, not enough for it to matter."

"Too much for me, just the same."

"Not much longer. I'm about to have an operation."

"Well, fine. Maybe we can get together again after you have it."

He came back several times. More than one girl was taken in by him, and not all of them turned him down.

Some of those drag queens are so feminine, so feline, such cats that lesbians sometimes get tempted by them.

What kind of relations do they have? Whether operated on or not, it makes no difference. For the nonoperated don't use their male genitalia anymore. Morally, they're castrates. Their only fun and only orgasm are mental. There is merely an interplay of fondling and tenderness, rather than any true sex act.

They are often unhappy. Refugees from one sex who have never really made it into the other, they sport a physical and moral emptiness, try to live in that other universe—woman's—which they would so much like to be part of. Mostly, they don't succeed, since women can't accept them as one of them. Sexual DP's, those who have been operated on as they age tend to become embittered old fat biddies, and very often commit suicide, since they can't abide the loss of the only value they ever had: their beauty.

What ever happened to Michel, that little decorator with the harmless physique, who besieged me for several nights? He was going to be operated on a few months later, once his hormonal and psychoanalytic treatments were over. He, at least, was being careful. He was trying in advance to program his future life as a woman: he wanted me to be a dominant mistress, whose abject slave he would be, for he was afraid of being forced to assume the initiative in the feminine role he so yearned for. He would have wanted to land on our shore with a mate already picked out.

"You'll be able to do anything you want with me. I'll be your most submissive, most obedient woman. Oh, if they'd only hurry and take off that horrifying blob of flesh I have between my legs, that monstrosity of nature. I'm a woman . . ."

Perplexed, I kept looking at this nice boy in his business suit, who kept on raving. For once, I was speechless.

There is another type of "character," who is sometimes referred to as being a male lesbian, or "queer for women," that is, a man who likes to wear women's clothes, make up and mince about, but is not a homosexual. He goes for women exclusively and likes to play a passive role with them, making love like a tortoise that has been turned over on its back.

Once, a long time earlier, I had met in a bar up in Montmartre a former cavalry officer, a captain who was a fine specimen of manhood, six feet tall with a Bourbon nose and in the prime of life. He dressed like an old-fashioned courtesan: a boat neckline revealing his bulging bust, a little pleated Indian skirt from Monoprix, a Himalayan wig, eye shadow and Baiser lipstick. He was an abomination, a caricature of a drag queen. Continually crossing and uncrossing the long legs he was so proud of, he expatiated about how he loved to make love to a woman, but *like* a woman, keeping his girdle on as long as possible so she wouldn't divine his sex. He loved lesbians exclusively, as disgusted as I with straight women, "because they stink of the male." He was a total—ridiculous—male lesbian.

I looked at this grotesque, painted-up scarecrow, who talked of his ludicrous conquests: cheapjill dykes, poor man's lesbians. And I tried to see him as the haughty spit-and-polish officer he had once been, who must have had no trouble in seducing almost any straight woman with his impressive military appearance.

Sometimes I attended interesting social dinners. One evening I was invited to the home of the chief operating officer of a big metallurgical company. Our host wore a girdle and garter belt beneath his trousers at board meetings, and at home entertained his guests in a white miniskirt and black boots. He isn't handsome or young, is rather swarthy, and looking at him is no delight. Yet he thinks himself irresistible. That night he had planned a "women's" dinner: with Maud de Belleroche, breathtakingly effervescent, and "Emmanuelle," very retiring, very Asiatic in her reserve. A supremely erotic dinner, with the conversation hopping gracefully from bed to bed.

Naturally, we discussed eroticism and pornography. We all three agreed on how ridiculous pornographic books were. They are all written by men, for men. The minute they mention the clitoris, for example, they become totally grotesque.

Our clitorises swell, enlarge, go into erection, flood sheets, mattresses, and bedside rugs, when they "ejaculate," they're the Styx, the Pactolus, and indeed, why not even "the Red Sea when it bleeds," like Cyrano's famous proboscis?

In short, they have us acting just like men whose penises had been worked on by Jivaro headshrinkers. Man wants to occupy even our organs, even our orgasms.

Well, we agree that this "miniphallus," this "stump" that makes us "sex cripples," according to Dr. Freud and his French disciple, Mlle. Bonaparte, this organ is important, but it is not the whole works. If we lesbians have the reputation for being exclusively clitoral, it is because all women are sensitive to that sort of caress, and we caress better than men.

All bisexuals will tell you: men do not know how properly to do oral honor to the sex of women. Barring those who are lucky enough to be initiated early by a partner who taught them how.

When people say that we are "failed" women because we were fucked badly, I just smile. We are on the contrary the best fucked of women and the ones who fuck the best.

For nothing is so grotesque as the argument used by men who want to convert and convince us at any cost: "Anything a woman can do for you, I can do for you just as well!"

"Just as well" remains to be seen! And even if that were so, once sated, once fulfilled, if I in turn wished to go down on the creature who had just made me happy, what would I find? A peak where I was seeking a soft shady valley, a stupid flat plain where my palm would like to englobe two breasts, and often, as an extra added attraction, useless, meaningless hairs. Thank you, I'd rather caress my dog.

How difficult it is for men to admit this.

I am always delighted when I catch the slightly irritated surprise of men at the sight of a couple of beautiful, feminine women together.

At the Microthèque there were two delightful girls who played up to me shyly and charmingly. They looked a bit alike, little blond pages of twenty-two.

Pascale raised monkeys and mice in the lab where she worked. Claude was a stylist. And she was the one who won out, perhaps because of her deep, rough, monotone voice that sent shivers up my back, perhaps because she was less bashful than Pascale. So I took her home with me one morning when Josette's war thunder was safely put away under lock and key.

Claude had known only two women before me, a saint and a whore. The saint had taught her very little, and the whore had turned her stomach and shocked her. She was just getting over that shock. Each further gesture when I wanted to pursue my lovemaking was met with a start, either distaste or modesty. She wore my patience thin. Moustique, of course, my first mistress and accomplished professor, had been the one who taught me to play with myself. I was ignorant. I knew nothing about it, had never had the curiosity to try. Like all little girls I had of course, at one time or another, taken a mirror and tried to see inside my unknown sex organs. The advantage that boys have is that theirs are right out in the open. So much so that they very proudly display the little rootlet that seems to dangle from their trunk. We, poor girls, poor women, have no such thing to display, to wave, to shake.

The first time Moustique tried to get me to do this, I remained amazed, then refused. I rebelled, embarrassed, ashamed. Her hands and lips were enough to satisfy me. She did not get discouraged, beginning over several times, guiding me, initiating me, her hand placed over mine, until my shame disappeared. I learned to be intimate with myself, to love myself. And, a born teacher like her, I have forced my lovers to do this when they refused. A warm sweet victory.

To break down the taboos, the shameful secrets hidden in the warmth of the sheets. To dare to celebrate one's own body before the eyes of another, to bring one's own self to a different kind of climax. To remain kneeling, as if prostrated, before a girl friend. To see that body you love to caress now move on its own, see a hand go forward in always graceful gestures, never obscene, never unesthetic like the brutal male action that looks so much like the milking of a cow, in its motion, its instrument, and finally the spurt of milky matter. (This is what makes a cow's teat as esthetically disgusting to me as a male sex organ.)

There, upon our fleece, that perfect triangle, the hand rests, seems to quiver like the wing of a bird, moves to the rhythm of a butterfly beating its wings on the pistil of a flower.

With Claude, my demands became almost tragic. Acquiescing, but then racked with shame, she burst into tears.

Another time, it was the initiation to mutual simultaneous love, mouths between the clefts of each other's thighs, that upset her and made her uneasy for the whole day.

It was very nice to hear people say, "How beautiful your friend is." It made me happy, it was a good mark of distinction in the business of running a club, but now my bed was changed into a courtroom where I had to justify each gesture, each caress. Still, I felt neither like a Messalina nor like Sardanapalus!

I became aggressive and unbearable, and nonchalant, defenseless Claude let herself be abused in silence.

One evening, a small aggressive person with the round face of a baby and bright little mouse's eyes asked me to have a drink, then two, then several. She was named Aimée, and she and a girl friend ran the Prélude, a very select gay bar across from Chez Castel. She started courting me in a strange way, as aggressive as all the rest of her behavior, an attack courtship that forced me to defend myself against what was sarcastic, ironic, and disconcerting in it.

She irritated but intrigued me. Physically, she was not my type and scarcely seemed attractive. But because she was a very good customer, I agreed to have dinner with her. That's unusual: professional nightlife is sufficiently demanding so that most of us turn our backs on it the minute we go out the door. Apart from the fashionable restaurants where one has to be seen or where I enjoy going with friends, I rarely accept dinner invitations.

She took me to the Méditerranée. She knew just how to order: the Saran was iced just right, the lobster meaty, the strawberries aromatic, and her conversation, once away from the music, was interesting and amusing. For, since we have to spend our evenings talking over the din of a musical background, I am often surprised by tête-à-tête conversations (in which you can be heard without having to shout). I wasn't sorry I had accepted. She discreetly went off to pay the bill. When I saw her coming back, slim, narrow, elegantly turned out, if slightly too butch for my taste, I thought she wasn't so bad, after all. She spoke to the owner and a smile suddenly lit up his usually masklike face. Well, she did have charm, and a lot of it! The cause was heard: I would not hold out for long.

Claude was away on a trip.

Happy coincidence.

Very quickly, I fell in love with Aimée, whose name derives from love itself. To dare to have such a name and not change it had impressed me. Although I am quick to rename people, I let hers stand. I had given funny or pretty nicknames to Maïna, Cat, Claude, Gisou, Josette, and all of them had finally adopted them.

It was March when Aimée and I had met. Once again, it was the season of renewal.

Cat was in a bad way. She had fallen into the clutches of a dangerous Algerian woman, always plotting and involved in all kinds of shady deals, who went in for group-sex orgies with her husband. But she was very beautiful. I warned Cat. That woman was bad medicine. And she remained my protégée, ever under my wing. The real love I felt for Aimée did not interfere with my affection for Cat. But she was deeply in love. Her Algerian already had her jumping like a pet poodle.

I was beginning my season at Saint-Tropez. At Easter, there had been X's wedding. Long before his arrest and suicide, everyone had known that he forced drugs on girls unfortunate enough to be taken in by his money, his fine houses, and his Rolls-Royces. A whole charter of guests came down from Paris, Aimée among them. There was a monster bouillabaisse at Tahiti, then a Camargue-style wedding ritual in which the bald old man ridiculously carried off his young bride on a passive mare, followed by apéritifs at L'Escale, fireworks, an evening at the Caves du Roy, the whole works. It was disgusting and revolting, because one could sense how his malodorous money crushed everyone.

I was happy, because Aimée was along. She had some mysterious dates, secret meetings with her boss from Paris, adorable Jacky Iskander, with all his almond-green sails to the wind and Cartier chains swinging, she went out without me, and finally came to make an announcement: in the summer, she'd be coming down to Saint-Tropez to turn the Stéréo into a male gay joint.

I was dumbfounded. Out of love, she was doing something silly. The only reason she took over this dump was to be near me. The Stéréo was a sailors' dive. The setting was lousy, filthy, the banquettes broken down. But what the devil was she doing in that galley? . . .

She was to open at the end of June. In Paris, where we were together again after Easter, we still met secretly, for neither her lover, the cold, calculating woman who owned the Prélude, nor Claude knew about us.

I was seeing the latter less and less frequently but abused her even more ferociously.

Her docility disarmed me. I couldn't find any good reason for making a break and if I hurt her by pushing her around a bit, that would only be good for her later on in life: perhaps I could teach her to become a bit tougher . . .

CHAPTER

VII

Jacky Iskander, Aimée, Michèle, who had remained my deejay, and I left for Saint-Tropez in June. I had taken an apartment on the port, a whole floor with an insuperable view. Cat, who had just left for Paris, had spent a month in it. I found out her Algerian friend had lived there with her. Everything was unspeakably filthy. Olive, my monkey, whom I had left there, had free run of the apartment and the walls were covered with the traces of his hands and feet.

Cat had a little chum, an adorable gay boy who looked so much like her that people often thought they were twins. He had rented a small shop near La Ponche for the season, where he sold strange morbid dolls that he dressed in old lace and jet beads.

Two days after Cat left, surprised at not having heard from him, but having a key to his studio, a friend and I went over to see what had happened to him. The minute we opened the door, a suffocating smell assailed us. "Keep out," my girl friend yelled.

He was lying on the floor, swollen, black, his face twisted into a grimace. He had swallowed two bottles of sleeping pills after Cat left, saddened because she had been so engrossed in her Algerian that she hadn't even come over to say goodbye. He had phoned me in Paris to say how unhappy he was over what he said was that woman's evil influence on Cat, suggesting nasty things, nefarious habits, to me. He was at his wits' end: sweet, but weak, he was a little girl with all kinds of talent.

"You killed him," I told Cat harshly on the phone.

She came down for the funeral; just the two of us and his mother. The Saint-Tropez Cemetery, so bright when you look at it as a tourist, is as depressing as any other when you bury a friend.

I had a temporary wooden cross made, with just two dates on it, twenty years apart.

Cat stayed within my orbit a little longer. Thinner now, with a strange look, she carried out a fake suicide attempt, extorted a small Austin from me, promising to pay me back for it out of her earnings as a barmaid, got in behind the wheel, and disappeared.

I've never seen her again.

Falling lower and lower, her Algerian friend ended in the women's prison of La Petite-Roquette. Cat left Paris suddenly when her friend was released, fat and pasty, under a Bastille Day amnesty.

God knows what illicit traffic, what sorry denunciations, what sordid carryings-on were hidden behind that departure.

Cat landed at Avignon, waiting table in black skirt, white apron, and round tray on her palm, at some little *café-tabac*. Quite a comedown . . .

After that she worked in a small suburban bar run by an old friend of mine, Vicky, and her lover. They had lived together for ten years and earned this bar franc by franc.

It belonged to them jointly. They were legally partners, with "papers" and everything—something we usually skip doing anything about, since legality seems superfluous to us, considering the permanent illegality of our sexual arrangements.

Cat came between them. The friend asked Vicky to get out. But she hung on, refusing to sell out for the peanuts they offered her. Two years ago, at Easter, she was found dead with a shotgun blast in her skull. She was lying in the bar she hadn't wanted to give up. Vicky, my sweet happy old pal, dead before she reached thirty-five.

There were some thirty of us at the church service. Black minks, astrakhan coats, ambiguous elegance. As always, two or three dumbfounded members of the family, embarrassed at our being there and at our prosperity, however unostentatious. Lesbians ought to be buried outside the city walls at night—the way actors used to be in the olden days—so as not to shock the burghers.

Today Cat runs their Avignon suburban bar.

Being in love, I was worried sick over how Aimée would make out with her sailors' dive. It was miraculous! Thanks to Jacky, who had once been Coco Chanel's secretary and knew all the Upper Crust whether or not of gay persuasion, thanks to the superb bartenders she had hired who went around recruiting on the fashionable beaches, thanks to Aimée herself who is such a favorite with aging millionaire ladies, the Stéréo was off and running. It caught on even faster than the Yeti had the year before, because there are many more gay men than lesbians and the room was three times as big.

That season, she and I were the queens of Saint-Tropez. Columnists mentioned our two clubs as the "in" spots. At Saint-Tropez that year, you just had to be a homosexual—of one gender or the other—in order to be in the swim.

We had it all: money, love, sun, and even Olive, who greeted us when we awoke, having torn apart all the closets, rolled in flour so that he looked like a Louis XV marquis—or else dripping with oil seasoned with "herbs of Provence," as if ready for the spit!

What a wonderful summer!

My pal Nicky had come from Marseille. Her new friend, a schoolteacher like her, was pregnant up to her eyes. She had told Nicky, "I want a kid, so it might as well be my husband's [she was married, and had only recently been converted]; then I'll get a divorce."

The maternal instinct exists in lesbians as it does in other women. It is not always atrophied, even though we may not show it. Nonmotherhood is a matter of choice, but it does not rule out regret or longing.

I don't agree with those who want to raise a child alone, or with their successive lovers. It's a big enough responsibility to bring a new being into this topsy-turvy and disoriented world, without depriving it further of the reassuring balance of a true family unit, that is, a father and mother.

Sometimes it seems that lesbians decide to have a baby the way they might buy a cat or a canary, without thinking of the consequences or the responsibilities involved.

I've known many happy children of lesbians, just as there are natural gypsies. But they're not the majority.

The ones who make such a decision, if they are wise, wait until they are at least thirty. To give birth earlier may be only a passing fancy that is too unfair to a little one who never asked to be born. One should have reached one's own equilibrium in life, be professionally established, have sufficiently solid bases set so that a cradle can rest on it without harm.

Moustique, you will recall, had a daughter, Andrée, a memento of a deep-sea-diving lover. I am one of those rare ones who really don't like children, finding them noisy and troublesome. Moustique's daughter found that out. I pushed her around and slapped her; I was hard, almost cruel with that little five-year-old, who looked at me with her big dark eyes unable to understand my hostility.

Even though I wasn't in love with her mother, I resented the fact that she had not preserved her physical integrity. Andrée was the living reproach. Her mother, boyish though she was, had been crushed under a male, penetrated, plowed deep. In my eyes, the kid was like a giant spermatozoon, the very proof of original sin. I knew, for myself, that had I realized I was a lesbian before meeting Guy I should never have allowed a man to force his way into the secrets of my body, my belly. With all the severity, the blind exclusiveness, and the headstrong partiality of my twenty years, I held this against Moustique and, beyond her, against little Andrée.

As I grew older, while still no fonder of babies and their inseminators, I sometimes reproached myself for the cruelty of my youth. For a long time, I kept telling myself that somewhere there was a young woman who must really hate me, Andrée, whose childhood I had ravaged, and that bothered me; truly, my only remorse.

Last year, at the Katmandou, I got a letter that read:

> You surely don't remember me, Elula. I found your address in the magazine *Le Crapouillot.* I'm presuming to write you because you don't know what you meant to me when I was little. I admired you, and loved you, and have never stopped thinking of you. You are the one fine memory of my childhood.

It was from little Andrée.

She came to see me at the Katmandou. She is twenty-five, has been married, has two children, and now lives with another girl. Like her mother. Like me.

I was beside myself with joy at finding her again. Andrée relieved me of the one little worm that spoiled one slice of my memories.

Her mother had dragged her along from one affair to the next, leaving her at the Foundling Home, the way furniture is put in storage, whenever she got in the way. So little Andrée had picked out the mother she would have liked to have, and her choice fell on me. How desperate and lonely that little thing must have been to love the harsh young woman who was always punishing her.

How can people say that children intuitively know whether you love them or not? Andrée had not noticed any of my barefaced hostility; or else she had chosen to forget it, so as to fashion me into her ideal, her nostalgic image.

If she became a lesbian and is happy living with her two kids and her lover, she was following my example, not her errant mother's. Is that an exemplary story? Or an exception?

I know some who, horrified at reading this, would give up any idea of having a child. "To have a lesbian daughter? I should hope not!" How often have I heard that cry of revulsion.

Now, were I to have had a little girl—my mind not countenancing that I might give birth to a male—I would have devoutly wished for her to be. But then, that's because I'm at peace with what I am, happy, not ashamed of my life, my tastes, my loves. So I wouldn't be afraid to see my child lead the same happy life. That, alas, is not true of all of us "cursèd" women.

I had been talking about a wonderful summer and here now are all these children. Where was I? Oh, yes, Aimée and I were riding high and happy in Saint-Tropez in July. Before starting work in our respective clubs, after which we would meet again at the end of the night, we attended those very Tropezian institutions, "dinners" at sumptuous villas given by charming, or amusing, or merely wealthy, friends. The doors were beginning to open for me. It had taken a year for people to admit I was something more than just a cocktail waitress who had come up in the world.

Of course, if I had remained married to Guy I would have had my own sumptuous villa in the "gardens of Saint-Tropez," and could, like so many others, have had me a pretty girl from time to time, whether or not I had to hide her from my husband.

But instead, I had opted for women, for no compromises, for freedom of amour, love before money, happiness before honors.

I regretted nothing. Especially now.

With Aimée, life had become golden, she treated me as

no one before ever had. With her, it was love, sensuality, affection, intelligence, finesse, complicity, the easy life, the dream life.

Through her, I discovered everything: sumptuous gifts, elegant parties, jewels presented with love. I felt more a woman with Aimée than I ever had before; because I was coddled, sated, adored. What love, what passion she had for me.

At the end of August I returned to Paris to find a very different atmosphere at the Microthèque from the one that I had created.

The landlady, whom I had put quietly behind the cash register, which had been her place for a year, was now known to one and all as Loulou. She cut capers on the dance floor, and tried to be the life of the party—which, at her age and with her looks, was truly a joke.

I could almost hear what she was thinking, what had been germinating in her mind while I was away: "She's terribly expensive, and I've been doing just as well without her."

I knew that my walking papers were being drawn up, and that one night they'd simply be handed to me. I had never been jilted by a lover, and I wasn't going to be in business either.

At the first altercation I had with her boy friend, without giving him another chance to proclaim that "you dykes have just never been fucked real good"—when for a year it was these misfucked dykes who had kept him in funds—I told him I was through as of the end of that evening.

They didn't try to get me to change my mind, all too happy to be rid of me.

The next day I phoned a friend who for six months had been after me to handle one of his clubs that never seemed able to catch on. Despite the alluring conditions which he offered me, I had always turned him down because I thought

I owed that much to the landlady of the Microthèque. Even though I had no contract with her, as so often happens in nightlife as well as in The Life itself, the dependability of your word and ethical behavior constitute your reputation and your best references.

That very evening, I went to look over his Katmandou. Two days later, my invitations were on their way to every one in Paris.

A week after that, I opened up, with the Microthèque staff that had come over to me plus two former employees from Carroll's and the Pousse au Crime.

That was December 2, 1969.

In two weeks, the empty, deserted Microthèque was out of business. It was to reopen a few months later, with "la grande Eugène" running it, and very successfully. But its great drag show moved on to the Champs-Élysées very quickly, after a few disagreements between the director and his/her landlords.

The Microthèque went on the auction block. The landlady tried her hand at a small club on the Rue du Colisée, by way of competing with me. She barely lasted out the winter.

Ever since, I live at the Katmandou.

I say "live," because quite apart from the long hours you have to put in at a club if it is to retain its character, the Katmandou has become my *raison d'être*.

It is the place where, every night, I meet up with a thousand and one women. They are my Cleopatra's bath—their faces, their smiles, their intrigues, the nascent flirtations, fading loves, joyfulnesses, surprises, ambiences, those loves at first sight, those deliciously tired feelings, exhausting nights' ends, gang departures toward further fun to be continued elsewhere when the whiskey has been flowing a little too abundantly and no one wants to turn in yet.

My Katmandou is a very fine place. I'm very proud of it.

At the right, as you come in, is the long all-mirrored bar, and the Murano crystal statuettes of long slim intertwined women.

The three steps to the room itself, the black panels of light tortoiseshell, the red velvet banquettes.

Above the golden metal dance floor, red suns pierce through the corbeled ceiling.

On the mezzanine, pinball games, restful armchairs for lounging and talking, deep cushions for kissing, a garden of greenery at the end of a spiral staircase inside a cage of gilt tubing.

And wherever you look, the infinity of mirrors that dazzlingly reflect women and their beauty.

Gone are the sordid ghettos of old. Now, at night at least, we have our own place in the sun.

In the last eight years, how many are the women who have come to drink, dance, flirt, in this theater with its nightly new show, and me as its ever-present audience? I hear, I listen, I collect confidences. I counsel, I console.

And I talk, too, with the privileged, sparingly admitted, vouched-for men, who may enter only if they follow the rules of the game.

Those are simple: Never approach a woman you do not know, whether to ask her to have a drink or to dance (in fact, dance as little as possible, it takes up too much space), and, especially, never try to make a pass at one.

If I were to do any of those things to a woman in a straight spot, they'd inform me more or less politely that I had to cease and desist. So all I'm doing is guarding a privileged territory until the day comes when all of us are allowed to do anything, anywhere.

One day, a man who had been kept out by my doorwoman asked to speak to me. Politely, and courteously, he inquired: "Tell me, madam, how can you be guilty of such ostracism, when you're the ones who are always demanding equal rights?"

"When you let us into the Stock Exchange and the French Academy, sir, you'll be welcome at the Katmandou."

Since then, the Bourse has fallen. But still not the Académie.

Most of the men turned down are not so gentlemanly. After trying a friendly soft sell, they turn on their heels, muttering, "Go on back to your cunt-lapping, you slobs!" as if that were some punishment they were condemning us to.

Or else they say, "Don't be afraid." Why do they think we're afraid? Are they so overpowering? Do they take us for scared little rabbits hiding in our holes because the hunters are on the prowl? Why can't they understand that they don't scare us, they *bother* us, they're useless, superfluous, and we have no desire to display our kissing, our flirtation to their curiosity, like a show?

Gay male bars are really lucky, because they don't have this problem with "she-voyeurs." No woman wants to go and watch her husband rubbing up against another man, while she quietly waits at her place, with her bag in her lap, until it's time to take them both home to bed with her.

But men—Conquistadores, Invincible Armada . . .

Men—remember—the League for the Rights of MAN, the future of MAN, always and forever MAN. The ostracism starts in the language itself. In the world of Man the King, woman is just an unimportant rib, guilty of the original sin. Religion of priests, politics of males, phallocracy!

And man's grammar. In French, if there is one masculine-gender word in any list or enumeration, it determines the gender of the whole. Proper usage is: There were a hundred women and one dog (not bitch), and all of them (*masc.*) were satisfied. Or else: The thousand little girls and one little boy were all (*masc.*) wild (*masc.*) with joy. Well, millions of women are wild (*fem.*) with rage. The millions of lesbians in the world constitute a supercursed substratum.

It's rare to hear men say that lesbians revolt or disgust

them. While they may want to beat the shit out of a fairy, they're more interested in fucking the lesbian.

How we do attract them! I've never heard anything but wildly flattering descriptions of us—so esthetic, so nice, so gracious. And how disinterested that admiration is! When they talk, their eyes light up, their mouths begin to water, they can already taste what a fine morsel they envision.

I don't believe in true friendship between men and women. There are too many vestiges of colonialism between us. The situation has never been cleared up. We are still swimming in paternalism. So, add to that, the fact that we lesbians are a bit of hard-to-reach fruit . . .

Men can become very good pals, but that too is hard. Even with intelligent men, who have brains instead of semen inside their craniums, it is difficult to have purely comradely relations. They can never quite completely forget that we belong to the race of the conquered, and their friendship always has some kind of undertone of protectionism or condescension.

As a very feminine and not-too-ugly lesbian, I have met only two or three men in my life whose friendship was truly sincere and without ulterior motive. With all the others, there's the weather eye out for the opportune moment just beneath the surface. Their patience is endless, their ruses without number. They can be friendly teddy bears, or roll adoring lover's eyes, or act the partying pal. But they can never admit that we can *really* do without them.

Sometimes, to rile a woman who has ignored his advances, the street urchin as well as the bourgeois will call her a dyke. Excuse me, a "dirty" dyke, the way they say "dirty nigger" or "dirty Jew."

They see it as an insult, an offense, and that reassures them. If any female turns down the wonderful little treasure they're ready to shove into her, there has to be something wrong with her. That spares their vanity. They struck out because she's abnormal, like some kind of kook, a pervert, a syphilitic. So, insult her, or even feel sorry for the poor idiot who'll never know the joy of feeling a male body crush her. Let her go get sucked off somewhere else!

Of course, I've never taken any of that as an insult. Such hateful spite rather delights me, and I never miss a chance to answer those who treat us that way that if all men were like them, there'd be a hell of a lot more "dirty dykes"—which would be all the better for me and all the worse for them.

Is a woman who is not a lesbian upset by such an "insult"? No. Generally, she laughs at it. It's less offensive than to be called a whore. If the insulters think she's going to throw herself between their legs to prove them wrong, they are certainly in for a surprise!

The fact that men hate us, whether latently or overtly, is something we are always aware of. Men aren't good losers. They hate losing a territory. They can't understand being rejected, excluded. "What a pity!" a man will sigh, when he sees a pretty lesbian.

Why a pity? Because he has lost a fine prey, or because she has lost the chance to be really fulfilled and happy?

Women don't feel so exclusive or possessive. A woman friendly with a gay man doesn't reproach him for being what he is nor for going with another man, equally unavailable. But a man is outraged in his proprietary instincts: one girl lost is bad enough, but to realize that her friend, especially if she is pretty, is also outside his grasp is just too much.

A Marseille industrialist, a Parisian showman, or a Nice antique dealer known to be a homosexual will be socially acceptable everywhere. They may be sneered at behind their backs, men may condescend to them with a touch of irony, but in the final analysis they're so many fewer hunters, so many fewer tomcats to go after the pretty pussies. So, they can dance attendance on your wife or your mistress like nice lapdogs, especially since straight women just love the empathetic attentions of these harmless cavaliers.

But a lesbian physician, lawyer, or antique dealer is embarrassing. She is competition, the more dangerous in that she doesn't employ the same weapons, and to top it off may be highly desirable, making it all the worse.

Lesbians who really make it big in Parisian society are never fully lesbians. They are always open to the idea of being in the company of men, even in their beds, or, more often, of slipping into the marriage bed with them and their wives. Had I been willing to go along with certain couples, certain men, I would have established my place in the social sun ten, twenty times over already.

But the men who were interested in me never turned me on in the slightest. They would quickly tire of a lesbian who offered them only comradeship or conversation. That, they could get from their peers, other men. That is not the role attributed to women in the universal comedy. When we won't play the game, we're left on the sidelines.

It's fun to watch two little Bilitis-type dykes making one another, but it's not acceptable when they're two women of one's own social set, two respectable bourgeoises. They are thrown outside the pale of the phallocracy. They are an insult to hetero-coupling.

And what a bad example they set for the wives! The latter may start making comparisons, and these may not always come out to the advantage of the "His/Hers" tandem.

If the lesbian is "single," she may be more readily acceptable: she may always be a recruit for the next orgy. But once she says no, she's a pariah, a pervert obviously out to seduce the wife of the couple. Not to be trusted, not to be associated with, not to be included on guest lists: she no longer exists.

If she's friendly with the wife, people may talk; if with the daughter, she may lead her astray.

So, if we want company, want to feel the warmth of a community, we obviously have to create our own society with its own restricted areas, rules, and customs.

In order to survive, we have to be discreet, prudent, unobtrusive. Not make ourselves noticeable, lest we be shot down.

A lesbian schoolteacher? Sacked, with a red mark against her—as is her gay male colleague. Just imagine, the horror of it! We might contaminate the young people in our charge. Slip our ideas or our fingers into innocent, unsuspecting beings.

I know a great many lesbian teachers, and I repeat that every one of them acts as I did. Girls being debauched by boarding-school mistresses are material for two-bit porno novels. But a married male professor who has more taste for fresh young females than for his old lady will be much more easily forgiven. And the tragedy of Gabrielle Russier, hounded to death for her affair with a boy in her class, would have won her no public sympathy nor any defenders whatever, had she loved and seduced a girl pupil instead . . .

Lesbian civil servants? Marked down in red in the secret file that's kept on all bureaucrats, never to be promoted. The paperwork timeservers get on their high horses to defend "morality." That was what happened to Dominique, and, finally discouraged, she had to resign from the Internal Revenue Service.

A woman deputy, or a city councilwoman? Out of the question for me, even though I should have loved to be in politics. Everyone knows that the people "want" virtuous, worthy representatives who live irreproachable lives. Elect a dyke? Never! She'd drag Marianne, the symbol of the French Republic, off to Lesbos, all Frenchwomen would become contaminated and none of them would ever raise another boy to be a soldier.

Under the Fifth Republic there was a gay cabinet minister who went out cruising in his flag-decked official car, but that's the exception. And besides, he had such a beautiful wife that Mme. de Gaulle was sure he had to be straight. Several notorious gays were also elected to Parliament in one of the Gaullist landslides, but that was because they were swept in with their party ticket, not balloted for individually, and one of them was finally hoist on the petard of a fine financial scandal.

Lesbian newspaperwomen? Yes, there are some. But they are quiet about it, keeping it especially from their little lesbian colleagues, who would be the first to torpedo them to clear themselves, in that milieu where guts are ripped out with such fine teeth. A few exceptions just prove the rule, such as that woman fashion writer who was the lover of a great newspaper owner's wife and is now living with a woman novelist. But what class it takes, what presence, and what professional standing for one to get away with it!

A lesbian chanteuse? Sabotaged.

But if every gay male singer were hooted off the stage, there would hardly be a crooner or rock star left. Which doesn't keep the groupies from grouping nor the lady fans from panting moistly in their seats when these idols appear, even though they may have been in the clink ten times for going after the large-bores in the Bois de Boulogne and everyone knows their so-called "fiancées" are just fronts. No matter. The ladies still applaud those asexual would-be males twisting and groaning before the mikes.

Lesbian singers, if not driven to suicide, never get higher than the second rank, no matter how much talent they may have.

Back in the fifties, the statuesque chanteuse at Carroll's was the subject of so much gossip about the princesses and oil queens she made out with, that she never could become a star.

If another one did get there, at the same period, it was because she had a girl friend, also a singer, who was married to a producer and he was able and willing to put her over.

I personally know of three women singers whose careers were shoved onto the back burner because they dragged their lovers along to parties as well as TV rehearsals. I never heard such a thing held against any male singers, living or dead, regardless of how musclebound or made up the pretty boys tagging along in their wake may have been.

In 1954, Boris Vian, then director of a record company, in my presence told Barbara, who was at the Écluse, "You'll never make it all the way to the top, because you're too obvious a lesbian."

Dear, dear Boris happened to be wrong on both counts: Barbara did become a real star of songdom and the fact is she is not a lesbian. However, if she had been, what he said would probably have come true.

A lesbian actress? My biggest heartbreak was over a young actress who had just finished the Conservatoire. She left me for fear I would hurt her career; I was too well known not to be noticed, and already people were talking about our affair. She got scared.

Even today, although it may no longer be utterly indispensable to make one's way via the casting couch, a lesbian actress is at a disadvantage. I can speak firsthand only of the theater and TV. In movies, it's said to be even worse. There, a girl's ass is still her passport to many parts, and the girl who won't sleep with men is quickly marked.

I have a lesbian friend who is a production manager in a big film company. One day she was on the set arguing with the technicians' shop stewards. It was a tight professional discussion. Whereupon the star of the film arrived, an actor whose ugliness and snottiness were his stock in trade. He broke into the discussion, which actually was none of his business, and ended up by declaring, "Oh, well, you just can't argue with a dyke."

Just another one who can't stand a woman doing a "man's job," especially one he won't be able to "bang." There, now I'm "sounding off" in his lingo!

So those who have succeeded as stars or great actresses did so by carefully staying in the closet all their lives. They need more talent than the competition. They contract a cover marriage, outside the covers, that is, say, with their favorite screenwriter, or if they're really lucky they become the wife of a homosexual actor so they can cover for each other. But that's very rare.

To be sure, at the height of their careers, or when they start to decline, when they've nothing left to gain or to lose and start to write their memoirs it would be nice if they—I won't say waved a manifesto or even performed an act of faith—at least for once did not distort the truth. Instead of describing their occasional affairs with men, which most people won't believe anyway, they might, between the recall of two films, two plays, or two anecdotes, slip in the fact that at least once they were in love with at least one woman.

A lesbian writer? Not one of them admits to it.

Lesbian lawyer? Lesbian physician or, worse, surgeon, architect, company president? There are some, indeed many. Just as there are lawyers and doctors who are blacks. But they are looked down upon even more condescendingly. A straight woman who really makes it in a career is met with a smile, a lesbian with gritted teeth.

So, like the others, they're quiet about it, they pretend, hide their loves, transpose their private lives.

That creates the great misunderstanding: that lesbians hide the fact because they are ashamed. The shame is all on you who don't allow us, once behind closed doors, once in our own beds, to be happy in our own way!

Why not?

What kind of professions are there in which lesbians are not handicapped? High fashion? As buyers, representatives, saleswomen, photographers, models, stylists? Not really. This impinges on the realm of the gay men. They are the ones who decide what we should look like, and wear, and how our hair should be styled. They impose towering hairdos on us or soles for clubfeet. They disguise women, make women look ridiculous, and women take it . . .

Everyone knows a given couturier or hair stylist is gay. His career isn't harmed; on the contrary! But who knows that a certain high-fashion couturière happened to love women?

What model dares to come out as a lesbian? A few hotheads do, and they are quickly put on a restricted list. Because it's no fun to "work with a doll you can't ball with between shots," especially if you're going to be off in the Caribbean or Tahiti doing the shooting—is it, all you fine fashion photographers? I spent four years living with a model, so I know whereof I speak. Two or three girls are selected and invited to dinner. Whether they come across afterward may well determine the "booking." My friend, a divine beauty, goes on very few junkets.

A lesbian photographer or designer might get by, because it is the talent reflected in their negatives or sketches that sells, and their sales don't necessarily depend on their beauty or availability.

What other professions are left to us to practice? Hair-styling, yes, and the craft jobs in which you are dependent on no one and talent is the only thing that counts.

That's pretty restricted. And it's sad.

Oh, yes, I forgot: We can also work in gas stations, as taxi drivers, as waitresses in commissaries, or nurses' aides.

Salesgirls? More difficult. There's always that male buyer . . . Office clerk, stenographer? Remember the free-feeling head of personnel. If you're unattractive, you may get by, be overlooked, and then quietly climb some small ladder without interference. But if you're the least bit pretty, run, run, little pigs, for your inversion will just make your fruit that much more mouthwatering for being forbidden, and either you'll have to be served up on a platter or you'll quickly be cast aside.

If I had had a daughter, I would have trained her for an independent career that was sufficiently remunerative so she did not need the pocketbook of any fancy prickster. And, if I had been lucky enough to see her follow in my tracks and be a lesbian too, she would have had it made and I would be without concern for her.

A gay man can land alone anywhere on earth. In his address book he'll have at least one contact, perhaps several, who will show him the town, introduce him to people, pave the way for him professionally and sexually.

This is not so for lesbians. That kind of sexual freemasonry is something that we still cannot afford. We are too wrapped up in our own survival to be able to take care of our sisters. When your boat is shipping water, you don't take on passengers . . .

Our brothers in inversion are lucky, the hairdressers, couturiers, designers, decorators, actors, and singers. They have full-bodied solidarity. A Republic of Little Comrades. Press, radio, TV, records, movies, high fashion, hairdressing, millinery, theater—all are their uncontested and incontestable domains. Getting ahead often depends on hopping between the sheets, and they have more than enough choices among all those careers.

Straight women will still find a few seats at the banquet table; there are still enough straight males in those professions to help them on their way if they proceed by way of their casting couches.

But lesbians get only the remains.

For a young actress who loves women and would like to use the bed as a ladder will find only the following in Paris:

4 television producers (one of whom is quite beautiful)
5 women directors
2 impresarios (about to retire)
3 A&R women in second-string record companies
2 theater owners
2 decorators

Almost all of these, to be sure, hide under neutral colors and try not to let their girl friends make the transition from their bed chambers to their offices.

As long as we have not acquired within society the security that sufficient money or power procures, we will remain the poor relations of sex, having to get along on crumbs, forced to keep isolated from one another, and the weaker for not knowing how to unite.

My gynecologist is a woman, so is my physician, my dentist, my bank president. My legal counselor is a woman, as is my partner, my entire staff is female, I bought my apartment through a woman broker, get my records from a woman music dealer, and if I still buy ham from a man, it is only because I haven't found a lesbian delicatessen anywhere near by.

If all lesbians joined together, we'd be much stronger. Then, like the gay guys, we could be a society within society.

So let's be patient. Society is coming our way. Lesbian loves are becoming fashionable. Even beyond such specific titles as *The Girl with the Golden Eyes, Olivia, The Children's Hour, The Fox, The Illusionist, Une femme un jour, Les Biches*, and *The Killing of Sister George*, there is hardly a film or play any more in which the (male) author does not insert a scene between two women, at times, to be sure, sticking out like a sore thumb. It's the latest spice. So much the better for us. Audiences are now beginning to consider that "it" exists everywhere, much more universally than they once had thought. They're getting used to our existence, soon will tolerate it, then accept it, for it will no longer seem to them an ultrarare, laughable anomaly.

That is why I am against the militant "red dykes" and other such grouplets of sex extremists with their provocative actions. Shocking the bourgeois, picketing noisily on Montparnasse sidewalks, or kissing women bus passengers on the mouth are not things that are ever going to gain us any popularity or acceptability.

I personally had been very lucky. From the Spanish stage to the Moroccan cabaret, from the "teacher's lectern" in Marseille to the doorbells all over France, from the restaurant kitchen in the Vaucluse to the tiny Cannes *boîte*, I had now worked my way into the only profession in which my label might help rather than hurt me.

Even as I might consider it odd to find a vegetarian butcher, or a dietitian weighing two hundred and fifty pounds, so I think it most logical for a lesbian to reign over lesbian nightlife.

Now, at last, I no longer needed to hide, to pretend, to worry about losing my job or my raise, to feel I would be looked upon as some strange animal, nor hear people sneer or whisper behind my back.

My success is due only to the women who have been coming in ever greater numbers to the Katmandou. It overwhelmingly shattered all the attendance records of the Microthèque.

As at the Yeti, famous people come to my club, but my problem remains unchanged: While I may openly mention the men who are habitués (because they can only be accused of voyeurism or at worst of three-wayism), I have to avoid mentioning the women habituées. Unlike other leaders of the night, I can't boast about or publicize my clientele. It's irritating, frustrating not to be allowed to point with pride to one's success, not to be able to say, "Last night D.C. and M.C. were in the club . . ."

It's the more upsetting in that the well-known women who do dare to come and dance at the Katmandou aren't lesbians! The ones who are, are generally too terrified to come through my poisonous portals. They're the ones who are afraid for their reputations!

The women who come, then, are those who aren't afraid to be given a label they know to be false. They come with friends, girls or fellows, dance without being bothered or propositioned by ever-prepared overgrown boy scouts, talk, have a drink, watch a couple of pretty girls dancing together because they're nice to watch, and then are on their way.

In all of these nights, I've met only two women who told me they were frankly disgusted by seeing girls in each other's arms. They were ill at ease, upset, almost aggressive, the way most straight men are when they venture into gay men's bars. But they didn't go so far as to insult us, as the straight men would have done to the homosexual men.

Women who come in for the first time and are just discovering our world are intrigued, wanting to know why and how. But their questions never reflect the unwholesome or titillated curiosity of men. They ask questions simply because they're women, and everyone knows that women are curious!

Curiosity leads to interest, interest to experimentation, and the steps are not great ones. True, if we *really* want a woman, we rarely fail to get her.

But there is no longer any point in claiming that this is easy because we present no danger to women who are afraid of becoming pregnant. For a long time, that was the common put-down. Our offensives succeeded because they were inoffensive.

With the coming of the pill, the fear that was supposed to bring the quivering quail into our arms is a thing of the past. Motherhood has become a matter of choice, and the lesbian is no longer a substitute for the pill. Women are now free to make up their minds . . .

No. It's because we know "the art of Courtly Love." We still know how to take our time, how to go about it slow and easy with a patience and delicacy one rarely finds in men any more—for the days When Knighthood Was in Flower are long since past.

We are finally able to make time with many a woman who, at the start, was merely amused by our advances. Even when we're broke, we send them flowers, shower them with gifts, envelop them in such a storm, such a whirlabout, that they finally give in. And then the sweet complicity of convents, harems, girls' schools is quickly re-created, and it's just a step from such affectionate attachments to sex. They may not remain lesbians later on, but their recollection of it is never ugly, never bad.

On the other hand, straight women may often be afraid to

be seen with us. While a woman can be seen out with a man and not have people necessarily conclude that she's his mistress, if she's seen with a lesbian, the immediate conclusion will be, "She's one of them."

We are contagious—carriers of a form of "galloping Sapphism." So those who dare say they are our friends are rare. But the women who do are independent, intelligent, open, liberated from social pettiness—in a word, ideal friends.

That summer we were supposed to go back to Saint-Tropez, Aimée to the Stéréo and I to the Yeti. But the landlady of the Stéréo had figured the same way as the owner of the Microthèque: "She's too expensive, and it'll go just as well without her, now that the tone has been set."

So she had made a deal with the bartender, and Aimée was out of a job.

As for Jacky Iskander, he was now over at Castel's, and Gérald Nanty was running the Prélude.

So we decided to take over the management of a beach at Saint-Tropez, Aimée to handle it full time with me helping out while continuing at the Yeti. We were able to get a backer who bought us a private beach near Club 55, at Pampelonne, and we modestly named our strip "Diamond Beach."

To help run it, I once again called in my mother. Mother, who was no longer twenty, was married for the third time, to a nice old Swiss-German industrialist who was delighted to be transported into a whole tribe of Chinese and handled chopsticks like a real *nga-quê*. He adored Asia, having always dreamed of being able to go there. And now he had it right at home!

Mother had met him through the matrimonial want ads in the *Chasseur Français*. They had been married for eight years. Between her stepson, who was an Anglican pastor, and her daughter, who was a lesbian by both vocation and profession, it was a wonder Mother's almond eyes hadn't started to cross!

Both of them came down to help open the beach, repaint

the place, draw up the menu, and cook Chinese dishes. Mother and I were reminded of her first time as a barmaid in Casablanca in 1950. Here it was twenty years later, and it was all starting over again.

What if now, as I approached menopause, I were to tell her I had gone straight? Maybe my adorable little mother would have raised her eyes to the skies and sighed, "You certainly are the twisted one, aren't you?" But enough of such nightmare-fiction. June was upon us, with fine weather, and the first customers.

We decided that Diamond Beach would be a "closed" place, like a nightclub, that is, admitting only those we knew. It was a lot easier than we had anticipated. When we wanted to turn people away, all we had to say was that all the mattresses were taken, or that there was no food left.

The rest of the "beachies" thought we were mildly out of our minds. When you have to make your whole year's take in two and a half months, you can't afford to be exacting about the kind of shorts people wear or the beachbags they carry.

But we were, and it worked. All the lesbians came to Diamond Beach. The gay boys came, too, at least those who had had enough of the overcrowdedness of the beach they usually went to.

It was one amazing spectacle to see this beach with its groups of topless girls side by side with bunches of boys as handsome and lithe as homosexuals can be, yet one side of it never mingling with the other.

CHAPTER

VIII

SHE CAME INTO L'ESCALE WHILE I WAS HAVING DINNER there with my parents. She was with a bunch of friends.

Her black hair was pulled back, under a white ribbon. She wore no makeup and was dressed in a white tailored man's shirt, and jeans. She looked like a queen. I dropped my spoon (I was eating bouillabaisse). She was the one I had been awaiting for all eternity.

As the man at the next table was one of my customers, he and I exchanged a glance of complicity when we realized that we were both eyeing her as she went by. I leaned toward him:

"Do you know her?"

"No. But we will."

He in turn called to a mutual friend, a producer, who was sitting across the center aisle. My mother was talking to Aimée. Like a good Swiss German, my stepfather was keeping still. But I was no longer with them. I had to go to her. I had to get to know her, to talk to her, to exist for *her*.

Finally, the answer came: she was an actress, named Léa.

On the following days, she was nowhere to be seen.

Some friends were pouring drinks at the housewarming of their new flat in La Ponche. In the cellar rec room they had set up a veritable nightclub, with lighted dance floor and large bay windows opening out on the little port. It was a great party. Momo, my Paris deejay, was there too. We come in together. I grab her by the arm, and say, "Momo, look at that girl. Don't you think she's sublime?"

"You mean Léa?"

"What do you mean? Do you know her?"

"And how! Her mother's one of my cronies."

She gets up, goes over to fetch a fine fiftyish lady with platinum hair.

"Elula, this is Laure," she says, "Léa's mother."

"Madame, my congratulations. Your daughter is the most beautiful woman anyone could imagine."

"You ought to see my son. He's not bad to look at, either."

"Well, your son—to be truthful, I prefer girls . . ."

She was close by, with Indian braids that made her look even younger. Her mother calls her over, introduces us.

I am barely able to get out, "I was just telling your mother how beautiful I thought you were."

She smiles slightly, says thanks perfunctorily, and goes back to her friends. I had spoken to her! Spoken to her! That was all I wanted. I did not want her. One does not want a dream. And besides, I've never known how to pay court to women. I have always waited for them to take the initiative, make the advances. I have always adopted a passive attitude—which often found me ending up in arms that were not all that attractive to me. So, better to keep after the talkative, outgoing, likable mother.

I invite her to have a drink on me at the Yeti whenever she wants. I insist. She promises. Two days later, she comes in, with her daughter and a man. The Yeti is full. But I still fix them up with a table. Léa is wearing a black dress. Her bare shoulders are the color of copper, the color of gold. The family friend asks her to dance. She is long, supple, I hear her deep, hoarsish voice. This is not thinkable. She is just what I have always dreamed.

"Dance with me, Elula?" her mother asks.

"I was about to ask you, Laure."

Why as we danced, and I never took my eyes off Léa, did she keep talking to me about her daughter? Telling me they were more friends than mother and daughter, that all she wanted was for Léa to be happy, and if, for example, she were to fall in love with me, she would not object in the least.

I broke out laughing.

"You're completely delirious. Your daughter would never fall in love with me."

"Oh, you know, in life, one can never tell how things will turn out. I lived with a woman for eight years before getting married. If she takes after me, anything is possible—and I'd be just as happy if you were the one. You are beautiful, I like you, and you must surely know how to love those who are interested in you. She could do worse . . ."

It was a surrealistic conversation! Science fiction! Léa, nearby, was smiling coquettishly at the old geezer, who was obviously in love with her. We returned to the table, and I sat down with them. The rest of the customers, that night, might just as well not have been there.

We talked of one thing and another. She was beautiful and I kept looking at her.

The next evening, they were back, still with the suitor in tow. Léa seemed more relaxed than the previous night. She was becoming acclimatized, tamed. When the photographer came by, the four of us posed together. On one of the shots, for the fun of it, Léa laid her head on my shoulder.

How I looked at that picture! Léa smiling, sparkling, her eyes alive with gaiety. A loose strand of her hair is touching my cheek. My head is slightly bent, my smile forced, as if I were embarrassed. Embarrassed by a gesture that was only a bit of play, but which I so would have wanted to be meant.

I went up to Paris for two weeks. It was July. Paris was beginning to be empty. But there were lots of people at the Katmandou. I had brought the picture with me, and showed it to some of my intimates.

"Look," I said, "my Saint-Tropez fiancée. Isn't she divine?"

As I kept repeating it for a joke, I began to wonder: Why shouldn't she really be?

Her "make-believe" closeness was more than I had been able to hope for. She accepted me as a lesbian, and at the time that picture was taken, played at being in love with me. Why not in reality? But how should I go about it? How?

At forty, I was as much at sea as I'd been back in Geneviève's day, when I was in love with her but sleeping with Moustique, and wanted nothing but to make love to her in turn and hear her moan as I was moaning in Moustique's arms.

But I didn't even think of making Léa moan with my hands or lips. My desires, my fantasies did not go that far. I have never known how physically to desire a woman I loved. It is as if the bedroom mystery had to remain intact until its final outburst. I envelop the woman I love with a virgin's modesty.

Each time I truly love, it is my first love.

I came back to Saint-Tropez. That same evening, as I arrived at L'Escale for a cup of coffee, Léa and her mother motioned to me.

Now, Léa was wearing a white dress with gold braiding. At the place where her right breast rose there was an insolent, provocative beauty mark. Her hair was up, with that same rebellious strand still breaking loose, earrings that ended in two pear-shaped pearls, and once again she was the cynosure of the entire terrace.

"I've missed you," I said.

"So have I. We haven't returned to the Yeti. We were waiting for you to get back there."

"You're even more beautiful than the way I have constantly remembered you during these two endless weeks."

"You're very beautiful, too, and you know it," she said.

"I have a confession to make. I showed all kinds of people that picture on which you're close against my shoulder—and the girls were drooling with envy. I let them believe you were my latest conquest."

She started to laugh and leaned toward me. Once again, she put her hand on my shoulder, there at the Escale, in front of everyone, the whole world, all eyes and ears. I found out what her skin was like by putting my hand on her arm, with its down that caressed my sensation-hungry palm.

Aimée came along. I got up.

"I have to be going to work," I said. "Won't you stop by?"

"I don't know if we can. We're going to a party at the Italians'."

"Well, then, please do come in. Just to say a quick hello. It's right on your way."

Aimée turned in early; her work at the beach did not allow her to stay up all night. At the Yeti, I was waiting for Léa to ring. She came by at about three in the morning, with a long white cape thrown over her white dress.

"I'm just staying a minute. I was so bored at that party that I finally ducked out. But I do have to go back. Mother doesn't know where I've gone."

"Come in. Even if only for a minute."

"I can't come in by myself."

"I'm here, what are you afraid of?"

"Of you, of course."

"Please, stay just a while. You came alone into the wolf's maw. Now, watch out! I'm going on the make."

"Why not? It would be a welcome change from all those boring guys."

"I'm not much of a hand at courting. When I've said a hundred times that you're the most beautiful woman in the world to me, I'll just be able to repeat the same thing. You paralyze me completely. Near you, I feel as bashful as a schoolgirl, even though I'm an old lady . . ."

"Don't be silly! You're more beautiful and younger than I."

Léa, Léa! We go on exchanging these banal compliments. I would like to shine, appear intelligent, but I can only hold her hand and look at her. Yet I know that my eyes speak much better than my voice, and so does my smile, which I know is charming and I know how to use.

"Now, I really do have to go."

"Don't go back to those jerks who will flock around you like flies. Don't you like my line better than theirs?"

"Of course! It's so charming, so tender. But Mother . . ."

Fortunately, Laure walks in.

"I was sure I'd find my daughter with you. What have you done to her that now she dares to come into this den of iniquity all by herself, when I had to force her to come here with me the first time?"

"Don't be silly, Mother. It was normal for me to be reticent. I had never been in this kind of place, you know very well. I was a little disgusted and very, very scared."

"And now, Léa? Now are you scared? Are you scared of me? Or disgusted?"

She laughs. Her escape is into laughter. Mother and daughter leave arm in arm, accomplices, so tender toward each other that they look like a pair of lovers.

The next day, at the Escale, I tripped over a piece of iron that was sticking out. My right foot hurt badly. I limped making faces all the way to the Yeti. As the night grew on, the pain got worse. My foot was twice its normal size.

"I think I broke my foot," I told Léa and Laure when they came by for their nightly little visit. They didn't want to leave me that way. They took me to the hospital, Léa making me lean on her arm. There I was told to come back the next day for an X ray. Meantime, my foot was swathed in alcohol compresses.

Léa and Laure were very worried. I was delighted: I was the center of her attention!

Léa absolutely insisted on coming for me in the morning to take me for the X ray. I hopped step by step up the four flights to my studio; I was in great pain, but in heaven. She could not be totally indifferent to me. She, who seems so eager for frivolous pleasures, so self-centered, was going to give up a morning of sea and sun for me.

Aimée wanted to come along. I said no. She had to take care of the beach, and Léa could take care of me. Poor Aimée. I lived beside her but no longer could see her. Only by constant efforts was I able to hide this new love which devoured me body and mind.

At the doctor's, Léa seemed more worried than I. She had on an Indian dress, was barefooted, with her hair flowing freely.

"I'm afraid for you, Elula," she said.

"Afraid? Why? I may have a broken foot. So what? Don't you realize that it's allowed me to have you here with me, all alone, taking care of me? This is the finest day of my life."

She didn't believe me. Yet it was true. One of my most exhilarating moments. Dazzling surprise, joy supreme. I wasn't even thinking of my foot. I just sat there, waiting for the results of the X rays, looking at her, talking to her, at last alone with her.

I had three broken toes. Léa went to get the plaster, and wouldn't let me pay for it.

"Terrific!" I said. "For three weeks my foot will be covered with your first gift to me."

She took me back to the studio and absolutely insisted on helping me up. I was ashamed of my awkwardness, of the weight that dragged my leg down and kept me off balance. We got to the fourth floor both soaked with perspiration. I would have liked to drink the drops that formed on her forehead and upper lip. To dry her face, hug her to me, tell her I loved her.

But all I did was fall breathless onto my bed.

"I'll come see how you are tonight. Now, rest."

She leaned over and grazed my cheek with her lips. I was so sweaty I did nothing to keep her there. I closed my eyes and exhaustedly fell asleep.

The heat was torrid. Not a sound came up from the street in La Ponche. Only the beaches were alive at this time. The village just napped till sunset. No more sun for me. This damned fracture was a pest. What would I do with the Yeti, Diamond Beach, and the Katmandou? What lousy luck! Some chance I'd have in a race against all her wealthy or devious suitors, with that lump at the end of my foot and on crutches!

The exhilaration I felt that morning was gone. Farewell to my wild hope of fulfillment.

That evening, Léa popped in for a minute. There were almost a dozen people with me. I was being made disagreeably important, all of them contributing their own ideas about the cast, how casts get wormy in summer, gangrene sets in, all those comforting things people find to tell a person with a broken foot.

The very next day, I decided to go back to work, gimpy or not.

To the beach at noon, three hundred meters to navigate under the August sun with crutches that sawed right through my hands. When I got to the end of the tarred path and reached the sand, I waited for the cook or dishwasher to come and carry me piggyback over the remaining two hundred meters of sand. My arrival waving my crutches turned out to be the big midday showpiece. They would stick me behind the cash register, since I couldn't do anything else, and I stuffed myself, eating up the plats du jour left over from the day before, all of them swimming in sauce, of course—just what my figure needed!

At six o'clock, back to Saint-Tropez. It took acrobatics to climb up the four flights, and then again in the evening to go back down to get to the Yeti, where I stayed all night on a banquette, until coming home again at dawn. From the very first evening, Léa was there, waiting to drive me home. She insisted on helping me climb the stairs.

"No, please," I begged. "It's bad enough giving this impression of being an awkward invalid. But not to that extent, before you, when I would so like to be . . ."

I turned toward her seat and put my arm around her shoulders. My lips went to her cheek, and stayed there a long time. My mouth slowly slipped toward her lips and found its place upon them. We stayed that way for a brief eternity. Breaths intermingled, lips together. I went no further.

I think that after that I had wings on my cast when I went up the stairs. I had a chance: she had not pushed me away. Now I just had to bring her around. I will take what time I have to, I'm in no hurry, time does not count, I want my love, nothing else matters. And after all, maybe this accident was a fortunate break.

Every evening, Léa would come for me. She went out to her social events and then suddenly Cinderella would leave the ball to come to me. We would spend an hour or more in her little car, talking, kissing. I caressed her face, her neck, outlined her lips, her ears, with my fingers. That beauty mark that had so fascinated me I now covered with my lips, and Léa, head thrown back on the car seat, eyes closed, thrilled, started, and ten times a night exclaimed:

"How can one get turned on so by a woman?"

There was no question of our making love. Not one of my movements suggested that. I didn't want to scare off my light-o'-love, this quivering doe who night after night was becoming tamer. Even as I might be reaching intense states of arousal and tension, she was quite unaware of it. I wanted her to love me, not just for me to make love to her.

I could take my time. We both lived in Paris. She was free, twenty-two, and had had one lover who had left no trace. She was innocent, slightly naive, and let herself go against me with such childlike innocence that sex was far behind whatever I might be feeling toward her.

At the Yeti, oblivious to gossip, we hid out at the back of the club and gave each other long, knowing, loving kisses the whole night through.

The day they took my cast off, Léa was away for a two-day stay at her aunt's in Cannes. I was not to see her till the next day. But I couldn't hold still. She was coming home during the night, I knew, and I got into my car and went over there, intending to slip a note under her door, for her to find in the morning.

I got into their garage at the same time as Laure, who was coming in with a little faggot she was putting up.

"Give this to Léa in the morning," I told her.

"No. You come on in and wake her. It'll make her happy."

"At this hour? I wouldn't want to disturb her. I don't want to seem pushy."

"You're being ridiculous," her mother replied. "I know there's nothing that would make her happier. Come on up."

I followed halfheartedly. I went in. Léa was hiding under the sheets, nothing but one hostile eye protruding. Seeing me, she shouted with joy and opened her arms to me. I sat down next to her, and she threw them around me. She was warm, almost naked. She hugged up against me with newfound passion. She covered my face with kisses. Laure was in the living room having a drink with the boy. I was embarrassed about their being so near. I got up.

"Now, I'll let you go back to sleep," I said.

"No, no, not right away. I'm so happy that you came. Go on in, I'll be right with you."

She slipped into a djellabah and dragged me out on the balcony. Day was breaking over Saint-Tropez. It was a stupidly sentimental chromo setting. She wanted to see me down to my car. And in the bare concrete cellar, so dark and sinister, as we were kissing for the last time, she whispered, "I love you, oh, I love you."

I hadn't dared say that to her yet.

Two days later, she was leaving for Paris. I borrowed the room of Michèle, my deejay, for an hour. We wanted to be alone together, in a private place, to say au revoir. I pulled her toward the bed. I unbuttoned her shirt and at last my hand was able to go to her breasts, followed by my lips. She had round proud mounds, two amber fruits, bursting with sap. She shyly pulled down the zipper of my tunic. In my turn, chest bared,

I leaned over her. Our breasts met, their tips pushing erect. I quivered and crushed down upon her. I stifled her moan with my lips. Nothing more would take place. That, we had decided. We were not going to make love furtively in some makeshift kip. We had waited this long, we could wait some more. I did not want to spoil Léa's first impression.

I might perhaps be her only woman lover. I wanted to leave her memories only of beauty, of delicacy, of refinement. But for a minute there, it was a near thing!

My body turned liquid, I was prolonging our kiss. Her body undulated under mine. Her hands were behind the nape of my neck and I could feel her nails caressing me. My hand was on her breasts, her sides, her belly, her thighs, but never once did I try to get to the core where all passions unfold.

We went back out onto the Place de l'Ormeau. Her shirt was so mussed that she tied the tails high around her chest and rolled the sleeves up over her elbows. We had agreed to separate outside the door, so as not to get involved into life, with people, together again. We said goodbye on that quiet little square.

I went to the hairdresser's, still limping on account of my foot, just out of the cast, which remained somewhat tender. Coming back out, I passed the wharf. Léa was at Sénéquier's with her mother and a faithful swain. I beat a hasty retreat and went the other way before she could see me. I didn't want to break the charm, for us to see each other or talk together in the presence of others. I hid myself away at the Gorilla's, behind a newspaper, and watched her talk and smile. She seemed absent. She was lost in space and had to get hold of herself in order to reenter the conversation. She was still back with me. She was thinking of our hour of love, and there I was, twenty-five yards away, spying on her. It didn't last long. She left—this time for good? I saw her go by at the wheel of her little car that she drove like a racer. The next time I saw her, we would be making love.

That was to be on her twenty-second birthday. The twenty-one white roses and one red rose that I sent her that morning, without any card, she knew came from me.

Our first night together. She so beautiful, I so overwrought my heart is thumping down from my chest into my gut. Léa, Léa who is a woman, The Woman, Femininity and Beauty, Léa aroused, amazed, dazzled, fulfilled.

Laure, quickly filled in, was very happy at this outcome. Every two days, I had fresh flowers sent to her place.

As soon as she got back, Léa had a part in a play. Rehearsals, fatigue, panic, stage fright.

I had told her I wouldn't come to pick her up, since, unfortunately, I am too well known to show people to go unnoticed, and I didn't want to "compromise" her.

Opening night. I have read the play, thrown cues to her, I know her entrances exactly. I may be more afraid than she. This is her first real part. Just before she goes on, there is a hitch in the set change: I feel I am dying for her.

She comes on. She is wearing a white-and-gold dress and a white mink jacket. Her hair is done up high. She is superb, divine, breathtaking.

Aimée knows all about us. I couldn't hide it from her any longer. I'm in love, in love as I feel I never have been before.

I had told her about it one evening, without preparation, as always. Anyway, is there any way to "prepare" someone for the fact you no longer love her, and that moreover you love someone else? Can you prepare someone for having her heart torn out? Can you kill a person thoughtfully?

She remained petrified, after her first she-wolf's "No!" It was a long, desperate, heartbreaking outcry. I wept. I didn't wish to hurt her. I didn't want to leave her. I did not intend to go and live with Léa. With Aimée I had a home, we had made a life together.

Léa, I knew, at any rate, could not last very long. It was not conceivable that she could stay with me. She was too much a woman to be able to do without men, their attentions, she was too bourgeoise and "well bred" to accept living outside the society that she liked—and there was her career, in which the label of lesbian was not one of quality.

Aimée suffered, but she stayed on. With my usual consciencelessness, which gets no better with the years, I lived beside her and made long phone calls to Léa, even though I detest the telephone and think of it only as a way of imparting a bit of news or setting up an appointment on ultrashort waves.

We saw what we could of each other, afternoons, for in the evening Léa was at the theater and I at the Katmandou. On days when she had no performance, we often spent the night before together. One night when I was dying of impatience to get back to her at five in the morning, I blew out a tire at the Porte Maillot and kept on driving on the rim all the way into Neuilly. I didn't have the time to lose the ten minutes it would take to change the tire. That could be taken care of tomorrow. I felt too keenly how numbered my hours of happiness were.

At the theater, as a matter of fact, tongues were wagging already.

Léa had nicely dodged a pass from the director, then the leading man, and now from the producer. Yet they could see she had no lover dancing attendance. So beautiful a girl, strange thing, that . . .

And to make it worse, there was a large cast in the play, and one of the actors was a homosexual who knew me, as did the leading lady's agent. After two weeks, everyone was aware of the fact that Léa was going with me.

She laughed when she told me about it, but her laugh was hollow, and became more and more hollow as the days went by. She had to put up with allusions that offended and outraged her, that she did not feel even applied to her. She was not a lesbian; she just loved me. In her eyes, those were two totally different things. Little by little, she got panicky. I felt her imperceptibly stiffening, growing away from me. Our relationship was quietly crumbling. A slight chink here today, another there tomorrow. An evasion, a missed date, two different excuses for not having supper together . . .

I confided in Laure, her mother.

"Hang in there," she told me. "I can assure you there's no one else. She just isn't used to it. Keep at it. I would like to see you stay with her. She never had any beau who was as nice to her as you are."

And her brother, who was handsome and self-assured, now was on the make for me, too. A child of twenty-five. Grotesque!

I was lovesick. In the evening, at the Katmandou, my pain would suddenly suffocate me, press down on me so that I had to leave the table I was visiting at to go upstairs and sit down on one of the ottomans and cry. I would sob for a few minutes, blow my nose, redo my makeup, and go back down, smiling professionally. My customers didn't need to know, to go through it with me. No one comes to a club to hear the hostess complain. They come to have a good time or, if they're sad or unhappy, to have a few drinks and tell their own troubles. My place was to be the listener, not the one to spout her problems. Of course, there were a few ghouls or necrophiles who were interested, but they would have plenty of time to gloat and make meat of it when this love of mine was truly dead. For the moment, it was only being put to the test. I was now being made to stand trial before the High Tribunal of Conformism, of the bourgeoisie, the fear of what-will-people-say.

I did not pass muster.

Léa's play flopped, which didn't help her morale. I put on a costume evening built around the theme of sado-masochism. Léa came in a fringed buckskin miniskirt, buckskin halter, slave bracelets on her arms, and high buckskin boots. She was beautiful enough to flog, to take, to violate until death. A woman I knew who was a theater manager was there. She immediately cast her for her next play.

I thought I had scored a point: for once, knowing me had not hurt her, quite the contrary.

I was wrong. Two weeks later, just before Christmas, I could consider my fine love to be gone.

Fortunately, there was still Aimée. She had put up with it all, gritting her teeth. Now Aimée, who had put up with my happiness shamelessly flaunted before her eyes, had to put up with my sorrow that took the form of unjustified angers.

On Christmas night, Léa was especially distant, her brother especially pressing, her mother especially noncommittal. She too was gradually withdrawing, in the wake of her daughter.

When I got home, I threw a fit of rage over the absurdity of life. That handsome boy who all night had tried to get into me while I was only living, and dying, to be with his sister! The staff at the Katmandou had given me a large crystal vase as a present. Outside my house, I threw it to the ground and smashed it into a thousand pieces. It was my heart being smashed. And Aimée was the one to pick up the pieces.

This big crisis once past, I became reasonable. I dressed my wound. Léa was nice about it and did not turn completely away from me, for she had not left me for anyone else. She was leaving me because of what I was, because she was afraid of what it might mean to her career, because she was weak. Because for all that her mother was a nonconformist, and she herself seemed so independent, she had been born in fancy upper-class Neuilly and that was where she was going to live and die.

She is still as beautiful as ever. I see her on the screen and I see her off it. She has not married. She has few lovers and does not flaunt them. She still goes out with Laure, and when she comes to the Katmandou, or to my house for dinner, it brings me real joy. Whenever I look at her, my heart beats a little faster, and I still say, "You know, it's true that you're the most beautiful of women."

She still breaks out with her raucous laugh. A few weeks ago, seven years after we first met, someone at a dinner asked her what her most beautiful memory of love was. With only the slightest of hesitations, she replied, "Elula."

It was a surprise. The people there did not know . . .

That is what is important, what really counts. The memory one leaves, the memory one keeps. The wound is licked, the blood stanched, so that everything is clean and neat, and then, the pain turns into affection or friendship.

Dominique, with whom I lived for four years, has an apartment in the same building as mine. Our love is over, but intimacy and passion created indissoluble bonds between us.

I know where I will finish my life with her: in the Drôme Department, in the village I love so, where the cemetery on the hillside has such a fine view of Mont Ventoux and the Ouvèze River.

Dominique is very close to me, even though we sometimes don't see one another for several days. In our feelings for each other there can be no problems, no rivalry, no pettiness. We borrow everything from each other, exchange keys, and share all our secrets. If tomorrow either of us wanted for anything whatever, the other would be there.

After losing Léa, I turned back toward Aimée. She took me back into her arms, took me down to Agadir, gave me all of her love. But something had snapped in me. Six months later, I left her for Marie-Hélène. Which is another story, a very long, very beautiful, and complicated story.

Aimée also remained very close to me. She bought an apartment just a stone's throw from mine, and lives there with a delightful designer. She is happy at last, for our separation hurt her deeply, and for a while her bed was open to anything that happened along—anything feminine, of course, for Aimée has never known a man, as is also true of Dominique.

She and I too trust each other totally. I have the amazing privilege of leaving behind, when I go, more good than bitter feelings, more happy memories than bad.

Perhaps because things are always neat and open. I cut to the quick, it bleeds, but there are no infections, no filth, no pettiness, no bickering. I go to a new love and leave one that is dying. But, in any event, I do it out of love. I live under the rule of love. My entire life, all of my thoughts are devoted to the woman I love. And if it is not always the same one, each time it is the most wonderful one, each time is the first time.

I will always be Aimée's partner. And she will always be mine. That either of us should betray the other is unthinkable.

The deep happiness that we have achieved is that of affection, tenderness, and confidence. If our loves go badly, we know where we can find refuge, we know who will help us, console us, protect us.

What luck I have had, to have met and loved these two women, and never to have lost them! What a joy to be alive, to love woman, to love women, to talk about it with women, to work with women!

Aimée and I bought the Katmandou together. Or rather, it is Aimée who really owns it, but papers don't mean that much! She or I, it's the same thing. Only she is more of a businesswoman than I, who am concerned only with human contacts and relationships between people. So it was normal for her to become the one to take charge of the business.

She is one of those lesbians about whom people say, "She takes herself seriously." But what does "taking herself seriously" mean? To have a home, a balanced, peaceful life, a secure position, like anyone else? Can only a wedding band, a marriage certificate, and two different sex organs that fit into each other give a person the right to want all that?

Our ambition, our drive for professional and social equality are beyond any possibility of compromise. No little cock slipped to us as a sugartit will keep us happy, nor will we soften up after a "good he-man fucking," as that macho writer Jean Lartéguy might have you believe.

"Your fight," some say, "is the same as that of the women's liberation movement, so stop your bellyaching!"

No. Our aims are parallel, complementary, but their struggle is not the same as ours. Besides, why call it a struggle? I have only been trying to explain what we are, and I revolt against stupidity. I am not on the warpath. I don't want to lead battalions of Amazons to destroy hearths, families, and institutions, but only to make our kind known and for us to be accepted, without salacious little leers. Only to get the bell dropped from around our necks that warns people, "She's a lesbian," as it might, "He's a Jew" or "He is black."

The women's liberation movement, for which I have the deepest respect, is something else. It is a movement for *all* women, mothers as well as whores, lesbians as well as old maids.

Some say, "Women's libbers are all dykes."

There are some of us in women's lib, and why not? We are women first of all. The liberation of woman that the movement is after is not only sexual liberation.

If it sometimes seems that lesbians are at the head of women's lib, it may be because we are one step ahead of straight women: we have already liberated ourselves sexually. We long ago learned how to use deception, how to defend ourselves against attacks from men, from bosses, from colleagues, from society. More inured to the blows, more experienced at it, it is normal and logical that lesbians should go into the front line to lead this attack on behalf of all women.

Women, this "Fourth World," these underdeveloped beings, are just beginning to shake their manes. They are gaining ground only foot by foot, the reins are being held on to as long as possible. Nations have had to give up their colonies, now men have to give up theirs. The helot is finally coming to life. She is making a place for herself; but it's not easy.

So, what about us? We who have thrown men off our beds and expelled them from our bodies? What can we expect from a male-dominated society? What can we aspire to? Society rejects us, repulses us. At best, it ignores us. Everyone knows the story about poor old Queen Victoria, who was asked, after she had signed the law that would send male homosexuals to prison, "And now, Your Majesty, what about the women?"

"What about what women?"

"Homosexual women."

"There aren't any!"

That's it: there aren't any of us! No legislation, no prophet has ever thundered against us. We have always escaped the rigors of the law, because male legislators have thought only of punishing gay men. For once, our insignificance in the eyes of men turned out to stand us in good stead!

Once I had two women friends who were peacefully living together in a little studio near Saint-Germain-des-Prés, that neighborhood in which people are supposed to be more intelligent, more advanced, than in any other place.

One day, they found the following scrawled on their door in chalk: $1 + 1 = 0$.

That inequitable inequation properly sums up men's opinions insofar as we are concerned.

CHAPTER

IX

I'M GOING TO HAVE TO GET READY. IT'S TIME TO GO TO THE Katmandou and rejoin grace and beauty. I am often asked whether it's a bore to be there every night, as if I were going to an office or a factory.

But each time is different and every evening brings me a surprise, and enjoyment—or a bother.

There is the joy of seeing old friends again, the appearance of some new beauty whom I greet more warmly than the others, as I give her special attention and place.

The women who come there almost all know each other and almost all are my friends. I like them because they're lesbians, like me. I like them despite their sometimes cloudy moods, their nerves, their sorrows, their angers. I am sometimes told the club is too decorous, not erotic enough . . . True, the girls have lots of "decorum." They flirt, they kiss, but nothing more. I don't see why there should be. I am not running a convent, but neither is my club a whorehouse.

The Katmandou is a place for enjoyment, relaxation, meeting.

This is a far cry from the Dantesque vision that Colette creates in *The Pure and the Impure* of "virile, wealthy old women . . . accompanied by calculating, tuberculous damsels . . ." going to Montmartre cellars "that sheltered these restless women, haunted by their own solitude, who found cheering comfort between low walls, under the rough protection of a 'Madame' who shared their secret and inclinations . . ."

Colette condemned us without appeal!

Was that really the way it was with the lesbians of the turn of the century? Even if this sinister, sordid picture was then a true reflection of the hell we lived in, things have greatly changed. It is perhaps time to realize this, to make it known, and to speak of us in more indulgent, truer terms.

You ladies who know how to write, you ladies who are well-known writers, why haven't you done it?

You, madame, with your witty column and brilliant novels, why do you allow your true tastes to come through only in your slightly oversharp critiques of the other sex?

You, madame, who wrote such a delightful trilogy and whose turbulent feminine love affairs were the talk of Tout-Paris at the time, you, madame, who in after years, kept Françoise Mallet from getting an award for *The Opportunist,* because you considered her book "immoral"?

And you, madame, who are so intelligent and whose charm has a thousand times been your beauty, why not a single book, a single play, a single film?

As for Françoise Mallet, she could afford to push her *Opportunist* because in the meantime she had become Mme. Mallet-Joris and was making babies.

Ah, Madame George Sand—if you had but been exclusively lesbian, you would have had the courage and the talent to write about us!

No, Madame de La Fayette, even if you had wanted, you couldn't have made your *Princesse de Clèves* into a lesbian, for in your century when Brantôme's "fair and gallant ladies" were carrying on, she would have ended at the stake, burned as a witch, a succubus, and a ghoul, that unseemly word from which must derive most of those pejorative French epithets that men so often apply to us (*gousse, gouine, gougnotte, goudou,* and the like).

Why don't André Gide, Henry de Montherlant, Jean-Louis Bory, Yves Navarre, and Roger Peyrefitte have sisters? In the Screen Studies they did on the subject of homosexuality, Bory, Navarre, and Peyrefitte wrote that they were sorry to see there was no lesbian among them. That was nice of them. They might perhaps better have said, sarcastically, that they were right to prefer men: men have more courage!

The endocrinologist and psychiatrist of the day were there, with stretchers, armbands, and clinical explanations, ready to bring help to the incurable males. But nothing for incurable females.

Not one of you lady writers has dared. What did you have to lose, since you were already established? Oh, you turn my stomach . . .

Our literature is restricted to two or three confessional novels. I forgot to mention *Thérèse and Isabelle,* but after those schoolgirl affairs, Violette Leduc did not remain a lesbian. She loved men, came with them, suffered through them.

Kate Millett? A bisexual, not a lesbian. And she's an American.

The Well of Loneliness? It's over half a century old. It is an outdated kind of Bible, and besides, Radclyffe Hall was English.

Who even remembers the poems of Renée Vivien, while the *Songs of Bilitis,* those distorted loves of two little Greek trollops, sung by a man, represent to the general public the height of Sapphic poetry! What a joke!

The only literature actually featuring lesbians is to be found in porno shops. These blossoms in the manure are laboriously written for the use of unimaginative males, who really think that two women ejaculate when they have their orgasms and mount each other while wearing rubber prostheses, those Loch Ness monsters that everybody always talks about but no one has ever seen.

I know there are infinitely fewer women than men writers, painters, musicians, or sculptors.

The second-class race which for centuries we have been is just now beginning to attain its intellectual majority. It is barely a century since we've had access to secondary schooling and we have one hell of a lag to make up for! We'll have to wait for the next generation. Its girls are freer, more daring.

They will know how, I am sure; they will dare, I hope.

Men will simply one day have to accept that literary or artistic creation does not belong to them alone; for the time being, the only type of creation they do not try to keep us from but gladly allot to us as our privilege is the creation and spawning of their children.

How happy I am to be a woman, but how sad too that I, an awkward journeywoman, should have to write in the place of the great ladies ensconced in their untroubled fame, even if it means I have to "bear up" under the hoots and hollers of the ignorant, the obtuse, the hostile, and the mocking.

If just one lesbian, hidden in her hole somewhere in the deepest provinces, finds out through me that one can be a lesbian and still be happy, that there is neither shame, nor anguish, nor despair in our condition, then I will have won my challenge.

O, you Straight Master of the Universe, give the poor lesbian the right to survive out in the daylight. Give her the possibility of living without going underground, of being able to love without listening for sneers, of being able to work without being persecuted.

Grant us, Venerated Master, Potentate of the World, the tolerance that your society accords to gay males. Do not treat us any worse than you treat them. Grant us the right to live and die out in the open.

May we one day be considered human beings with full rights, and at last perhaps, may harmony be set up among the four sexes (male and female straights, male and female gays).

Give us the right to happiness which so many of us are seeking. For not all of us have my rage to live, my ability to find joy and happiness everywhere and at every moment. For not all of us are fortunate enough to be at peace with themselves and able to carry on the front-line fight, as I can, who have the time and the means for it.

Women, I thank you. Women, I am dying of love for you. My heart is not large enough, nor is there time enough, for me to be able to love you all, as I would wish to. Each of you is a lake into which I would like to immerse myself. Each of your sexes, each of your mouths is a temptation toward a slow death. I love you so much that I despair at seeing time go by. I am so eager for you that I throb to the stories of your lives, the details of your loves. I share them because they are also to an extent my own. All of your lesbian lives, the happy and the poignant, the successful and the shattered. Each day I learn to know you better, and to love you the more.

I would like to be your poet, to sing of you, but all I am able to do is to tell my own story—the story of a life that is in no way exemplary, except insofar as it is neat and clean as steel.